FILET CROCHET FROI

CENTER PIECE
Instructions on page 33.

TABLECLOTH

Instructions on page 34.

TABLECLOTH

Instructions on page 36.

TABLECLOTH
Instructions on page 37.

CENTER PIECE
Instructions on page 39.

TABLECLOTH
Instructions on page 40.

TABLECLOTH

Instructions on page 42.

PIANO THROW

Instructions on page 44.

TABLECLOTH

Instructions on page 46.

CHAIR BACK
Instructions on page 48.

ELEGANT CROCHET FOR

TABLECLOTH

Instructions on page 50.

WAGON MAT

Instructions on page 52.

CENTER PIECE

Instructions on page 52.

CENTER PIECE

Instructions on page 56.

TABLECLOTH
Instructions on page 58.

DOILIES

Instructions on page 58.

Instructions on page 62.

Instructions on page 65.

Instructions on page 64.

Instructions on page 64.

Instructions on page 66.

Instructions on page 67.

Instructions on page 69.

LACES MADE OF MOTIFS

TABLECLOTH

Instructions on page 70.

TABLECLOTH

Instructions on page 74.

TABLECLOTH

Instructions on page 77.

TABLECLOTH

Instructions on page 72.

TABLECLOTH

Instructions on page 71.

BEDSPREAD

Instructions on page 75.

Center Piece shown on page 1

You'll Need:
D.M.C crochet cotton #20, 6 20-gram balls White. Steel crochet hook size 0.90 mm.
Finished Size: 59.5 cm by 44 cm.
Gauge: Filet crochet; 22.5 squares = 10 cm, 21 rows = 10 cm.
Making Instructions:
Ch 298. Row 1: Ch 5, 1 dc in 9th ch from hook, * ch 2, sk 2 ch, 1 dc in next ch, repeat from * across.
Row 2: Turn (turn each row), 292 dc, end ch 2, 1 dc in 3rd st of beg ch.
Rows 3-7: Work dc and ch referring to chart.
Rows 8-125: Work straight, making patterns as shown on the chart. Make net pattern (repetition of "1 dc, ch 5" for the 1st row, "1 dc, ch 3, 1 sc in ch-5 1p, ch 3" for the next row) on corners.

59.5 = 125 rows

44 = ch 298 sts (99 squares + 1 st)

33

Tablecloth shown on page 2

You'll Need:
D.M.C crochet cotton #20, 20 20-gram balls White.
Steel crochet hook size 0.90 mm.
Finished Size: 116 cm in diameter.
Gauge: Filet crochet; 18 squares = 10 cm, 18.5 rows = 10 cm.
Making Instructions:
Motif: Ch 85. Row 1: Ch 3, 1 dc in 5th ch from hook, 1 dc each in each of next 83 ch, ch 12 to inc.

Row 2: Ch 3, turn (turn each row), 15 dc starting at 5th ch from hook, (ch 2, sk 2 sts, 1 dc) 26 times, 3 dc, inc 12 dc referring to chart.
Rows 3-9: Work as for row 2, increasing each side.
Rows 10-12: Beg with ch 3, 3 dc, *ch 2, 1 dc, (or 3 dc for the bl on the chart), repeat from * across, end with 4 dc. Rows 13-100: Work decreasing each side. Dec beginning side working sl st, dec ending side leaving sts. Make 8 motifs, joining to previous motif where marked.

Motif (8 pieces)

Joining to previous motif where marked. (Reffer to chart)
(● =manner-a)
(○ =manner-b)

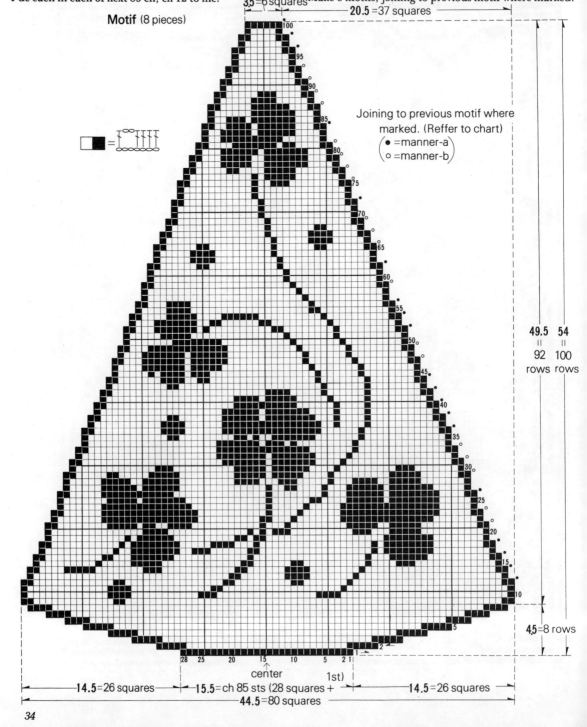

Center part of crochet, joining

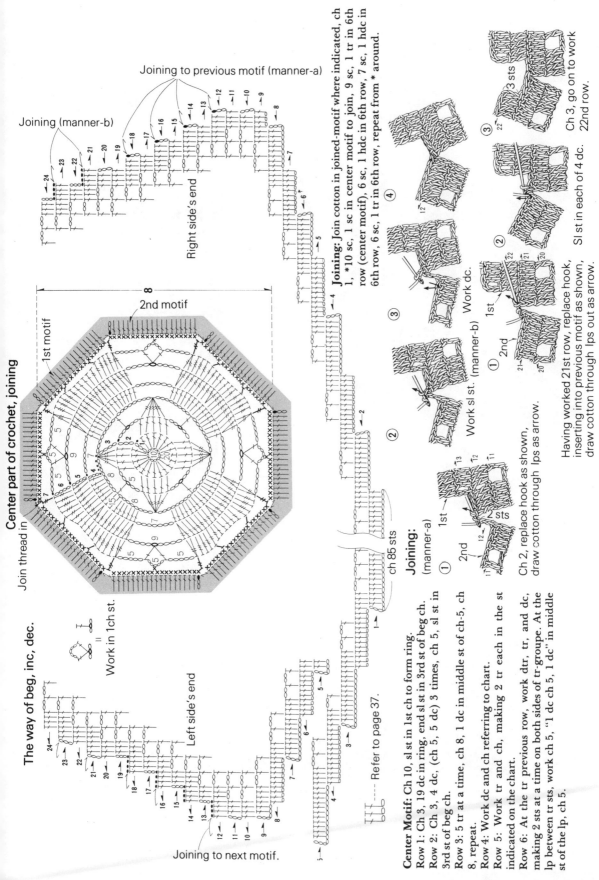

The way of beg, inc, dec.

= Work in 1ch st.

Join thread in

1st motif

2nd motif

Left side's end

Joining to next motif.

Right side's end

Joining (manner-b)

Joining to previous motif (manner-a)

--- Refer to page 37.

ch 85 sts

Joining: Join cotton in joined-motif where indicated, ch 1, *10 sc, 1 sc in center motif to join, 9 sc, 1 tr in 6th row (center motif), 6 sc, 1 hdc in 6th row, 7 sc, 1 hdc in 6th row, 6 sc, 1 tr in 6th row, repeat from * around.

Joining:
(manner-a)

Ch 2, replace hook as shown, draw cotton through lps as arrow.

Work sl st. (manner-b)

Work dc.

Having worked 21st row, replace hook, inserting into previous motif as shown, draw cotton through lps out as arrow.

Ch 3, go on to work 22nd row.

Sl st in each of 4 dc.

Center Motif: Ch 10, sl st in 1st ch to form ring.
Row 1: Ch 3, 19 dc in ring, end sl st in 3rd st of beg ch.
Row 2: Ch 3, 4 dc, (ch 5, 5 dc) 3 times, ch 5, sl st in 3rd st of beg ch.
Row 3: 5 tr at a time, ch 8, 1 dc in middle st of ch-5, ch 8, repeat.
Row 4: Work dc and ch referring to chart.
Row 5: Work tr and ch, making 2 tr each in the st indicated on the chart.
Row 6: At the tr previous row, work dtr, tr, and dc, making 2 sts at a time on both sides of tr-groupe. At the lp between tr sts, work ch 5, "1 dc ch 5, 1 dc" in middle st of the lp, ch 5.

35

Tablecloth shown on page 3

You'll Need:
D.M.C crochet cotton #20, 20 20-gram balls White.
Steel crochet hook size 0.90 mm.
Finished Size: 115.5 cm by 91 cm.
Gauge: Filet crochet; 20 squares = 10 cm, 19 rows = 10 cm.
Making Instructions:
Ch 547. Row 1: Ch 3, 6 dc starting at 5th ch from hook, (ch 2, sk 2 ch, 1 dc) 8 times, * 24 dc, (ch 2, sk 2 ch, 1 dc) 9 times, repeat from * 9 times, 24 dc, (ch 2, sk 2 ch, 1 dc) 8 times, 6 dc.
Rows 2-8: Work as for 1st row referring to chart.
Rows 9-107: Inc or dec on sides following chart. Make patterns symmetrically.
Rows 108-214: Work as for previous rows, making patterns symmetrical to top half.
Edges of Top & Bottom: Join cotton in where indicated on the chart, work 3 rows of filet crochet.

91 = ch 547 sts (182 squares + 1st)

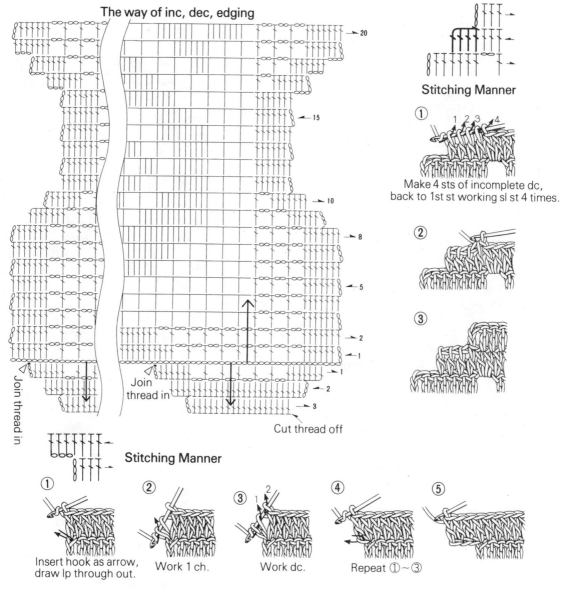

The way of inc, dec, edging

Join thread in

Join thread in

Cut thread off

Stitching Manner

① Make 4 sts of incomplete dc, back to 1st st working sl st 4 times.

②

③

Stitching Manner

① Insert hook as arrow, draw lp through out.

② Work 1 ch.

③ Work dc.

④ Repeat ①~③

⑤

Tablecloth shown on page 4

You'll Need:
D.M.C crochet cotton #20, 19 20-gram balls White. Steel crochet hook size 1.00 mm.
Finished Size: 117 cm by 107 cm.
Gauge: Filet crochet; 17 squares = 10 cm, 17 rows = 10 cm.
Making Instructions:
Ch 562. Row 1: Ch 3, dc in each of 561 ch, starting at 5th ch from hook.
Rows 2-84: Work making patterns as shown on the chart. Ch 2, 1 dc for each sp, 3 dc for each bl. Make net pattern (repetition of "1 dc, ch 3 1 sc, ch 3" for the 1st row, "1 dc, ch 5" for the next row) in the middle 4 places.
Rows 85-167: Make patterns on up half and on down half symmetrical, except net pattern.

Border: Row 1: Ch 4, *ch 5, 1 4-dc puff, repeat from * around, making "ch 5, 1 tr" at corners, end sl st in 4th st of beg ch.
Rows 2-3: Work as for row 1.
Row 4: Dtr in each st around, making 7 dtr in corner st.
Row 5: 1 sc, 1 ch-4 p, 5 sc, repeat.

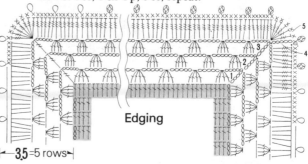

Edging

3.5 =5 rows

100 = 167 rows

130
120
110
100
90
Center
80
70
60
50
40
30
20
10
5
1

110   100   90   80   70   60   50   40   30   20   10   2 1

Center

110 = ch 562 sts (187 squares + 1st)

Center Piece shown on page 5

You'll Need:
D.M.C Crochet cotton #20, 8 20-gram balls White.
Steel crochet hook size 0.90 mm.
Finished Size: 64 cm in diameter.
Gauge: Filet crochet; 20 squares = 10 cm, 20 rows = 10 cm.

Making Instructions:
Loop end of cotton. Row 1: Ch 3, (ch 1, 1 dc) 9 times in lp, ch 1, sl st in 3rd st of beg ch.
Row 2: 1 dc in dc, 2 dc in ch-1, repeat.
Row 3: Inc working "1 dc, ch 1, 1 dc" at 10 places indicated on the chart.

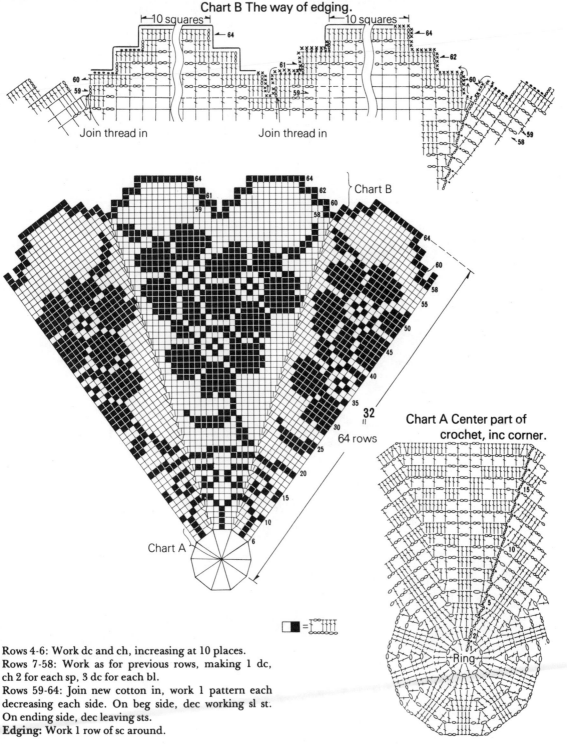

Chart B The way of edging.

Chart A Center part of crochet, inc corner.

Rows 4-6: Work dc and ch, increasing at 10 places.
Rows 7-58: Work as for previous rows, making 1 dc, ch 2 for each sp, 3 dc for each bl.
Rows 59-64: Join new cotton in, work 1 pattern each decreasing each side. On beg side, dec working sl st. On ending side, dec leaving sts.
Edging: Work 1 row of sc around.

Tablecloth shown on page 6-7

You'll Need:
D.M.C crochet cotton #20, 37 20-gram balls White. Steel crochet hook size 0.90 mm.
Finished Size: 153 cm by 115.5 cm.
Gauge: Filet crochet; 22.5 squares = 10 cm, 23.5 rows = 10 cm.
Size of Motif: 35.5 cm by 35 cm.
Making Instructions:
A-Motif: Ch 241. Row 1: Ch 5, 1 dc in 9th ch from hook, *ch 2, sk 2 ch, 1 dc, repeat from * across.
Row 2: Turn (turn each row), work as for row 1.
Rows 3-82: Work straight following chart (ch 2, 1 dc for each sp, 3 dc for each bl). As for the net pattern in the middle, work 1 dc, ch 3, 1 sc, ch 3, repeat from top for the 1st row, alternate 1 dc and ch 5 for the next row. Make 6 motifs.
B-Motif: Ch 241. Make 6 motifs in same manner as for A-motif.

Joining Motifs: Make 3 rows of 4 motifs. Alternate 1 sc and ch 3 (ch 5 on corners) around the 1st motif. From 2nd motif, join to 1st one working sl st at the middle of each 1p.
Border: Row 1: Alternate 1 sc and ch 2 (ch 1 on corners) around.

Chart of Measurements

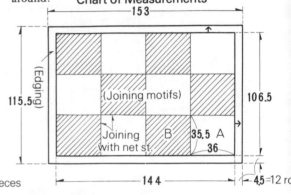

Motif A 6 pieces

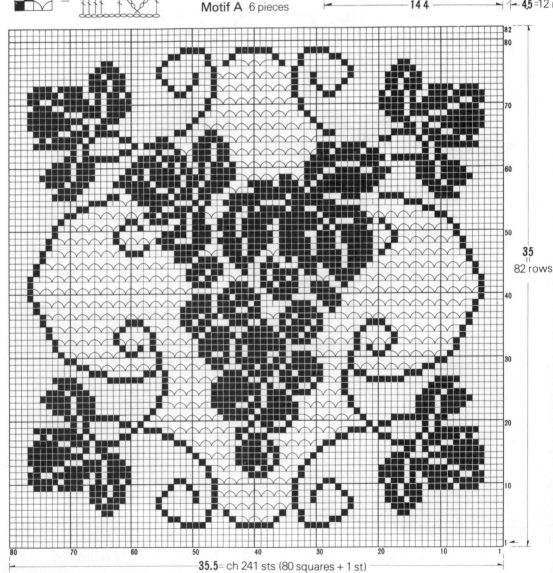

35 = 82 rows

35.5 = ch 241 sts (80 squares + 1 st)

Row 2: 1 dc, ch 3, 1 sc, repeat,
making 1 dc, ch 5, 1 dc at the corner.
Row 3: Alternate 1 dc and ch 5
around, making 1 dc, ch 2, 1dc, ch 5,
1 dc, ch 2 at the corner.
Rows 4-11: Work as for rows 2-3.
Row 12: Sc in each st around, making
ch 1 at the corner.

The way of joining motifs, edging

= Crochet dc in bold

Motif B   6 pieces

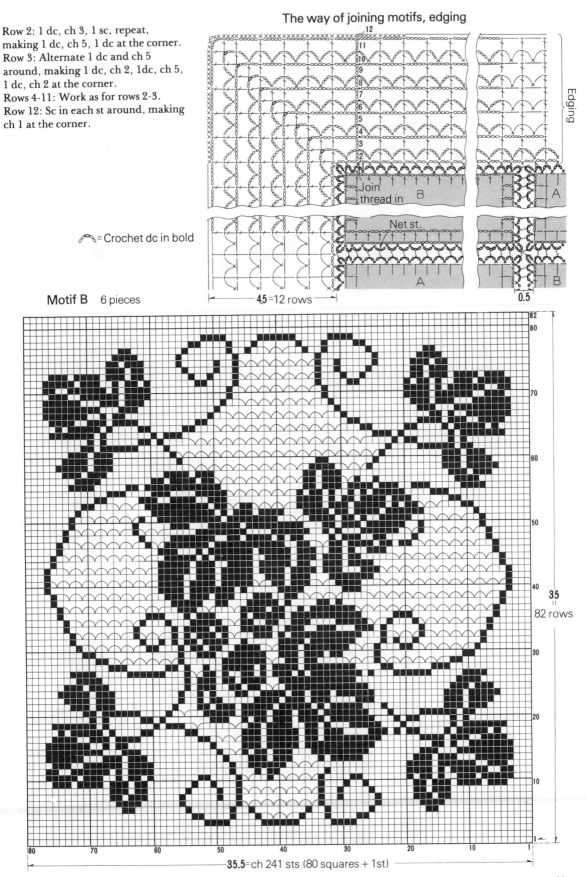

35.5=ch 241 sts (80 squares + 1st)

35
=
82 rows

Tablecloth shown on page 8-9

You'll Need:
D.M.C crochet cotton #20, 32 20-gram balls White.
Steel crochet hook size 0.90 mm.
Finished Size: 154.5 cm by 109.5 cm.
Gauge: Filet crochet; 20 squares = 10 cm, 20.5 rows = 10 cm.

Making Instructions:

Ch 634. Row 1: Ch 5, 1 dc in 9th ch from hook, * ch 2, sk 2 ch, 1 dc, repeat from * across.

Row 2: Turn (turn each row), work as for row 1.

Rows 3-309: Work straight, making ch 2, 1 dc for each sp, 3 dc for each bl.

Border: Row 1: Alternate 1 sc and ch 7 around, making "ch 3, 1 tr" instead of ch 7 at the corner.

Rows 2-3: Net st of ch-7 (1 sc, ch 7) around.

Row 4: Alternate net st of ch-3 and ch-7 around, making ch-5 at the corner.

Row 5: 2 sl st, ch 3 to form 1st st, ch 1, 2 dc in 1p, ch 3, 1 sc, *ch 3, 2 dc in 1p, ch 1, 2 dc in same 1p as last 2 dc, ch 3, 1 sc in next 1p, repeat from *around, end 1 dc in 1st 1p, sl st in 3rd st of beg ch.

Row 6: "(1 dc, ch 1) 2 times, 1 dc, ch 3, (1 dc, ch 1) 2 times, 1 dc" in ch-1, ch 3, repeat.

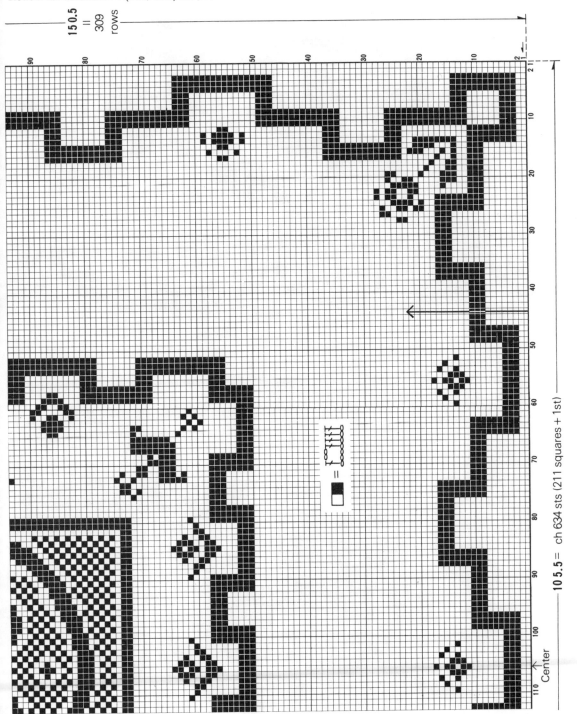

43

Piano Throw shown on page 10

You'll Need:
D.M.C crochet cotton #20, 14 20-gram balls White. Steel crochet hook size 0.90 mm. Light weight White linen 157 cm by 40 cm.

Finished Size: Refer to chart.
Gauge: Filet crochet; 20.5 squares = 10 cm, 24.5 rows = 10 cm.

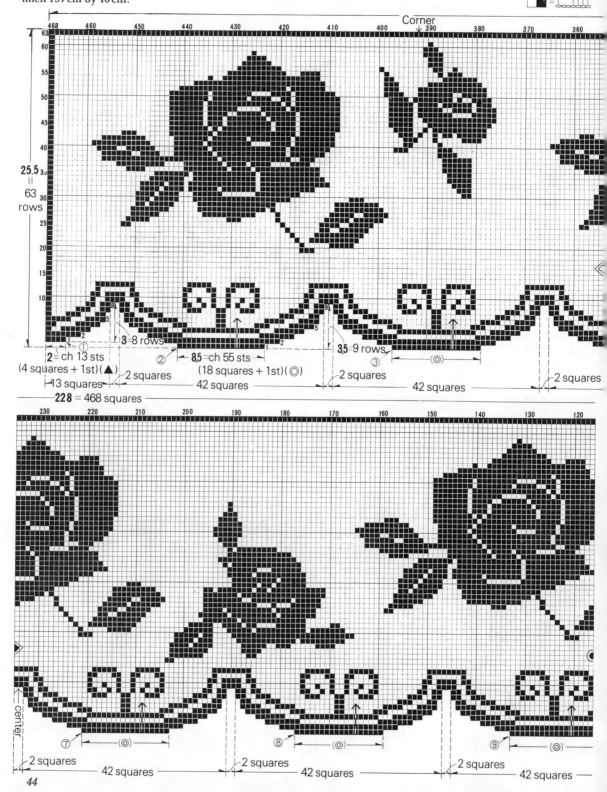

Making Instructions:

Work in numerical order.

①: Ch 13. Row 1: Ch 3, 12 dc starting at 5th ch from hook, ch 9.

Row 2: Ch 3, turn (turn each row), 21 dc.

Row 3: Work dc and ch referring to chart, inc 6 dc at the end.

Rows 4-8: Work as for rows 2-3, increasing one side.

②-⑪: Ch 55 respectively, work 9 rows as for ①, join to adjacent groupe, making ch 5, 1 sl st.

⑫: Work 8 rows as for ①, ch 5, join to 9th row of ⑪ making 1 sl st.

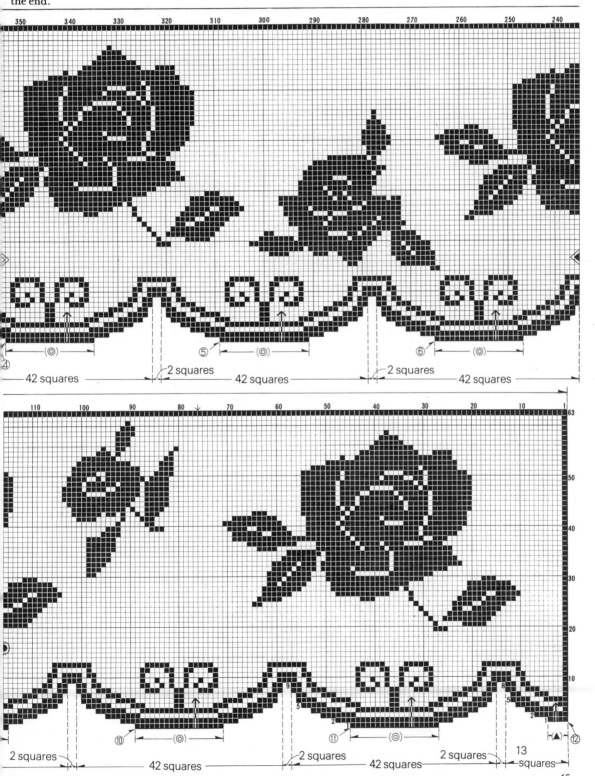

45

Rows 10-63: Work whole the row straight. Work 1 dc, ch 2 for each sp, 3 dc for each bl.

Edging: Work along top edge. Ch 1, 1 sc, * 3 dc, ch-3 p, 3 dc, 1 sc, repeat from * across, making a corner at the place indicated.

Finishing: Fold back raw edges of linen twice, slip stitch steady, place edges of lace over, sew steady.

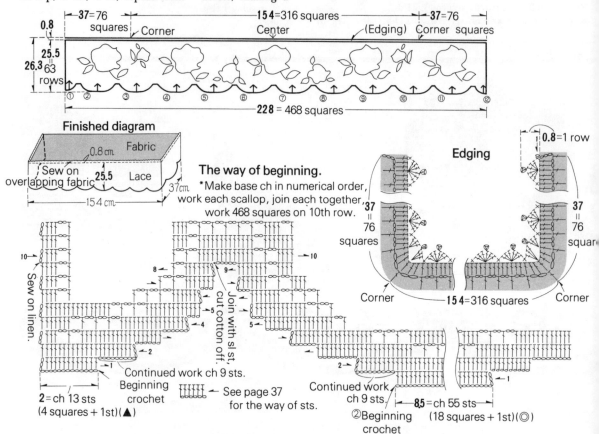

Finished diagram

The way of beginning.
*Make base ch in numerical order, work each scallop, join each together, work 468 squares on 10th row.

Edging

2 = ch 13 sts
(4 squares + 1st)(▲)

See page 37 for the way of sts.

8.5 = ch 55 sts
(18 squares + 1st)(◎)

②Beginning crochet

Tablecloth shown on page 11

The way of joining motifs, edging

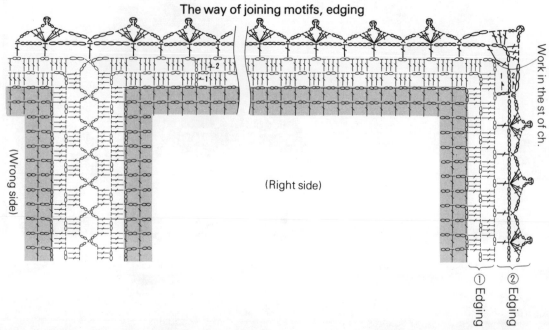

(Wrong side)

(Right side)

① Edging

② Edging

Work in the st of ch.

You'll Need:
D.M.C crochet cotton #5, 50 20-gram balls Beige. Steel crochet hook size 1.25 mm.

Finished Size: 136 cm by 120 cm.

Gauge: Filet crochet; 15 squares = 10 cm, 16.5 rows = 10 cm.

Making Instructions;

Motif: Ch 118. Row 1: Ch 5, 1 dc in 9th ch from hook, ch 2, sk 2 ch, 1 dc, repeat from * across.

Row 2: Turn (turn each row), work as for row 1.

Rows 3-213: Work straight referring to chart (ch 2, 1 dc for each sp, 3 dc for each bl). Repeat design (each requires 50 rows) 4 times. Make 4 motifs in same manner.

Edging-(1): Work along each motif. Row 1: Alternate 4 dc and ch 2 around, making ch 5 instead of ch 2 at the corner.

Row 2: Work as for previous row. From 2nd motif, work joining to previous motif with sc. Join motifs front and back alternately together.

Edging-(2): Row 1: Alternate 1 dc and ch 5 around, working dc in corner st 2 times as shown.

Row 2: 1 sc, ch 3, "3 dc, ch 2, 1 ch-3 p, ch 2, 3 dc" in dc (in 1p at the corner), ch 3, repeat.

Chart of measurements

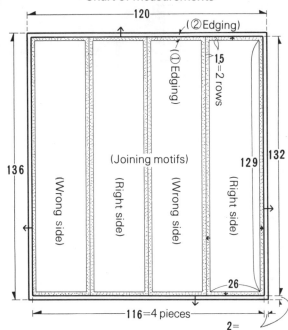

Motif (4 pieces)

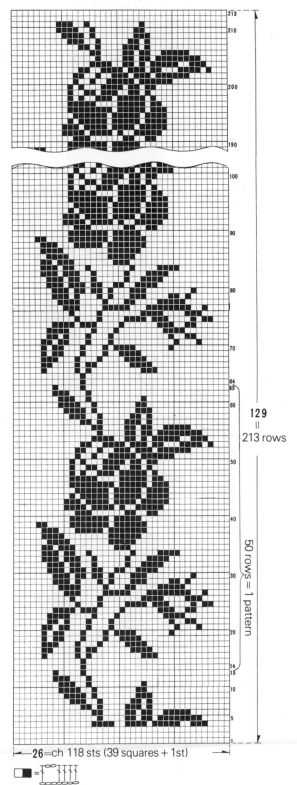

47

Chair Back shown on page 12-13

You'll Need:
D.M.C crochet cotton #5 White, 28 20-gram balls for main piece, 9 20-gram balls for small piece (for each). Steel crochet hook size 1.50 mm.
Finished Size: Main piece, 142.5 cm by 62 cm. Small piece, 62 cm by 38 cm.
Gauge: Filet crochet; 16 squares = 10 cm, 16 rows = 10 cm.
Making Instructions:
Main Piece: Ch 676. Row 1: Ch 5, 1 dc in 9th ch from hook, * ch 2, sk 2 ch, 1 dc, repeat from * across.

Row 2; Turn (turn each row), work as for row 1.
Rows 3-95: Work straight, making ch 2, 1 dc for each sp, 3 dc for each bl. As for the net pattern on both sides, alternate ch 5 and 1 dc for the 1st row, work ch 3, 1 sc, ch 3, 1 dc for the next row.
Border: Row 1: Ch 5 at the end of row 95, alternate 4 dc and ch 2 across, 1 dc in 1st st of base ch, ch 3 to form 1st of the row, 2 dc in cross side of last dc, 1 dc in 1st st of base ch, ch 2, repeat.
Row 2: Repeat row 1.
Small Piece: Ch 172. Work as for main piece.

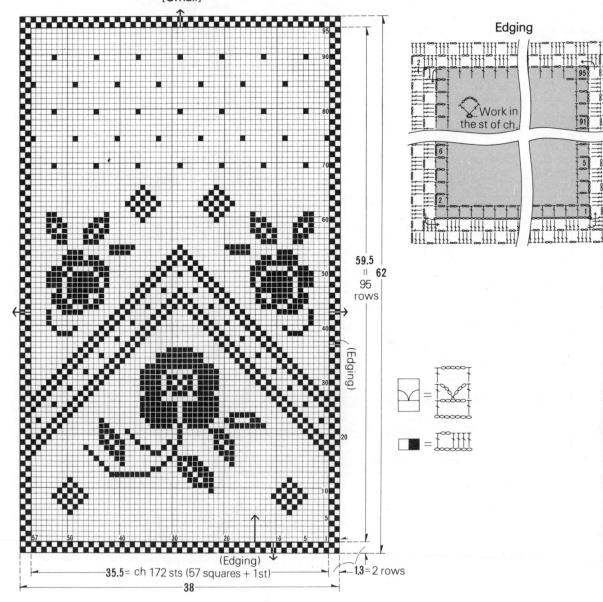

[Small]

Edging

Work in the st of ch.

59.5 = 62
95 rows

(Edging)

(Edging)

35.5 = ch 172 sts (57 squares + 1st)
38

1.3 = 2 rows

62

59.5 = 95 rows

1,3 = 2 rows

1,3 = 2 rows

(Edging)

(Edging)

1,3 = 2 rows

[Large]

140 = ch 676 sts (225 squares + 1st)

142.5

Center

49

Tablecloth shown on page 14

You'll Need:
D.M.C crochet cotton #20, 19 20-gram balls White.
Steel crochet hook size 0.90 mm.
Finished Size: 125 cm in diameter.
Gauge: 1 row of tr = 0.8 cm.
Making Instructions:
Ch 8, sl st in 1st ch to form ring. Rnd 1: Ch 3, 23 dc in ring, sl st in 3rd st of beg ch.

Rnd 2: Ch 5 to form 1st st, ch 2, * 1 dtr in dc, ch 2, repeat from * around, sl st in 5th st of beg ch.
Rnd 3: Alternate 3 tr and ch 2 around.
Rnd 4: Alternate 3 tr at a time and ch 5 around, end working "ch 2, 1 dc" instead of ch 5.
Rnd 5: In middle st of each 1p, work 2 times of "1 tr, ch 3".
Rnd 6: Repeat rnd 5, increasing sts of ch as shown.

Rnd 7: "5 tr, ch 4" in ch-3 1p.

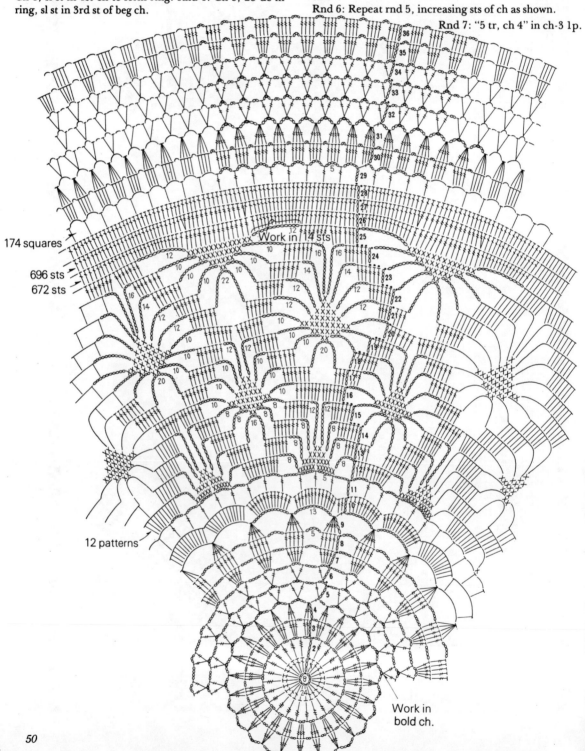

174 squares

696 sts
672 sts

12 patterns

Work in 14 sts

Work in bold ch.

50

Rnd 8: 1 tr each in each tr 5 times, ch 6, repeat.
Rnd 9: 5 tr at a time, ch 13, repeat, end working "ch 10, 1 dc" instead of ch 13.
Rnd 10: 10 tr each in each 1p around.

Rnd 11: 1 tr, ch 5, repeat.
Rnd 12: Ch 4 to form 1st st, * ch 8, 1 sc in tr, 5 sc in lp. 5 sc in next lp, 1 sc in tr, ch 8, 5 tr in lp, 1 tr in tr, 5 tr in next lp, repeat from * around, end 4 tr in last 1p, sl st in 4th st of beg ch.

14 sts.   13 sts   14 sts   14 sts   13 sts   14 sts   14 sts   13 sts   14 sts

Work in 7 sts each 29th, Chains.

35 patterns
210 squares
1050 sts

51

Rnds 13-25: Work as for rnd 12.
Rnd 26: Dc in each st of tr and ch, tr in each st of sc.
Rnd 27: Dc in dc, tr in tr, making 2 sts each in edge st of the groupe of tr.
Rnd 28: Dc in each st around.
Rnd 29: Alternate 1 tr and ch 5 around, end working "ch 2, 1 dc" instead of ch 5.
Rnds 30-31: Work as for rnds 3-4.
Rnds 32-34: Work as for rnds 5-6.
Rnds 35-54: Work as for rnds 7-26.
Rnd 55: Ch 6, 2 tr tr at a time, * ch 5, 9 sc, 1 hdc, 13 dc, 1 hdc, 9 sc, ch 5, 3 tr tr at a time, repeat from * around, end ch 5, sl st in the st of 1st 2 sts at a time.
Rnd 56: Tr in each st around.
Rnd 57: Ch 4, 3 tr in same place as ch 4, ch 13, sk 14 tr, "4 tr, ch 3, 4 tr" in next tr, ch 13, sk 13 tr, "4 tr, ch 3,

4 tr" in next tr, ch 13, repeat in same way around, end 4 tr in same place as beg ch, ch 1, 1 hdc in 4th st of beg ch.
Rnds 58-59: Work as for rnd 57. When to work the sc on 59th rnd, wrap the lps of 57th and 58th rnd together.
Rnds 60-71: Work as for rnds 57-59.
Rnd 72: Ch 8, "(1 dtr, ch 3) 2 times, 1 dtr" in lp, * ch 10, "(1 dtr, ch 3) 6 times, 1 dtr" in next lp, repeat from * around, sl st in 5th st of beg ch.
Rnd 73: Sl st to proceed to the middle of lp, ch 5, 1 3-dtr puff, ch 5, 1 4-dtr puff in next lp, ch 5, 1 3-dtr puff in next lp, 1 sc in the midle of ch-10, continue in same way around. Sure to make 3-sts puff on both sides of each sc.

Wagon Mat shown on page 15

You'll Need:
D.M.C crochet cotton #20, 4 20-gram balls White.
Steel crochet hook size 0.90 mm.
Finished Size: 75 cm by 34.5 cm.
Gauge: 1 row of dc = 0.5 cm.
Size of Motif: Refer to chart.
Making Instructions:
Motif: Ch 18, sl st in 1st st to form ring.
Rnd 1: Ch 3, 35 dc in ring, sl st in 3rd st of beg ch.
Rnd 2: Ch 3, 1 dc each in 5 dc, (ch 6, 6 dc) 5 times, end working "ch 3, 1 dc" instead of ch 6.
Rnd 3: Ch 3, 1 2-dc puff, ch 3, 1 3-dc puff, ch 9 * (1 3-dc puff, ch 3) 2 times, 1 3-dc puff, ch 9, repeat from * around, end working "ch 1, 1 hdc" instead of ch 3.
Rnd 4: Referring to chart, work dc and ch around, making "1 dc, ch 3, 1 dc" in middle st of each ch 9.
Rnd 5: Ch 3, * (2 dc, 1 ch-3 p, 2dc, 1 dc in dc) 2 times, "2 dc, 1 ch-3 p, ch 2, 1 ch-3p, 2dc" in ch-3 lp, 1 dc in next dc, repeat from * around.
From 2nd motif, work rnd 5 making sc in previous motif as shown. Join 44 motifs together.

Work in the st of 1 ch.

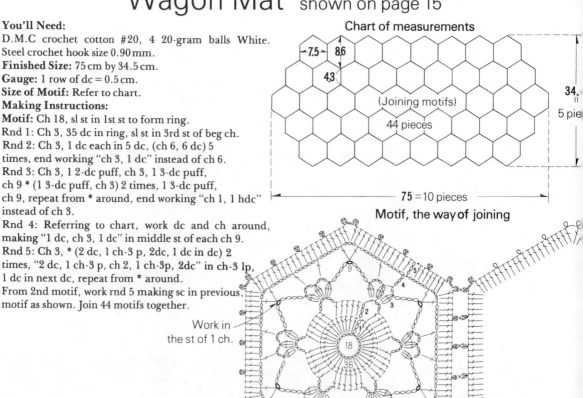

Chart of measurements

7.5 86
4.3
(Joining motifs)
44 pieces
34.
5 pie

75 = 10 pieces

Motif, the way of joining

Center Piece shown on page 16

You'll Need:
D.M.C crochet cotton #20, 4 20-gram balls White.
Steel crochet hook size 0.90 mm.
Finished Size: 55 cm in diameter.
Gauge: 1 row of dc = 0.6 cm.

Making Instructions:
Loop end of cotton. Rnd 1: Ch 3, 23 dc in lp, sl st in 3rd st of beg ch.
Rnd 2: Ch 3, 1 dc in same place as ch 3, 2 dc each in each dc around.

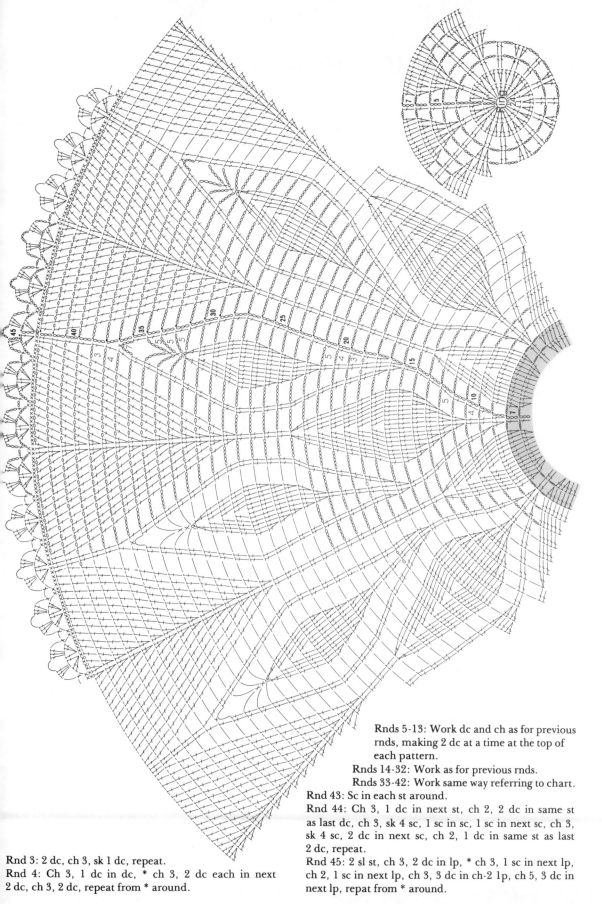

Rnds 5-13: Work dc and ch as for previous rnds, making 2 dc at a time at the top of each pattern.

Rnds 14-32: Work as for previous rnds.

Rnds 33-42: Work same way referring to chart.

Rnd 43: Sc in each st around.

Rnd 44: Ch 3, 1 dc in next st, ch 2, 2 dc in same st as last dc, ch 3, sk 4 sc, 1 sc in sc, 1 sc in next sc, ch 3, sk 4 sc, 2 dc in next sc, ch 2, 1 dc in same st as last 2 dc, repeat.

Rnd 3: 2 dc, ch 3, sk 1 dc, repeat.

Rnd 4: Ch 3, 1 dc in dc, * ch 3, 2 dc each in next 2 dc, ch 3, 2 dc, repeat from * around.

Rnd 45: 2 sl st, ch 3, 2 dc in lp, * ch 3, 1 sc in next lp, ch 2, 1 sc in next lp, ch 3, 3 dc in ch-2 1p, ch 5, 3 dc in next lp, repat from * around.

Center Piece shown on page 17

You'll Need:
D.M.C crochet cotton #20, 5 20-gram balls White.
Steel crochet hook size 0.90mm.
Finished Size: 54 cm in diameter.

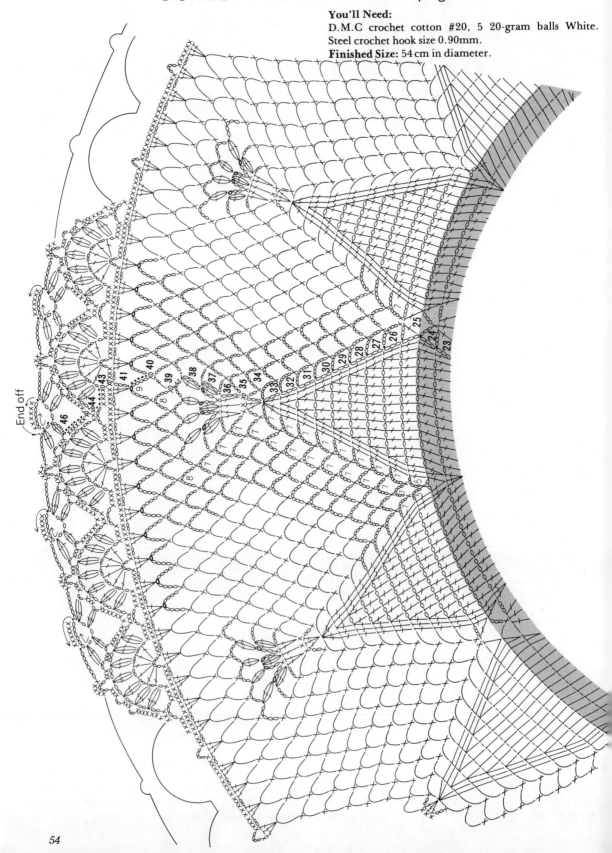

Gauge: 1 row of dc = 0.6 cm.

Making Instructions:

Ch 6, sl st in 1st ch to form ring. Rnd 1: Ch 3, 1 dc in ring, (ch 2, 2 dc) 7 times, ch 2, sl st in 3rd st of beg ch.

Rnd 2: 2 sl st, ch 3, 5 dc in lp, 6 dc each in each lp around, sl st in 3rd st of beg ch.

Rnd 3: In each st around, make 2 dc and 1 dc alternately.

Rnd 4: 9 dc, ch 3, repeat.

Rnd 5: "ch 5, 1 sc, ch 5" in each ch-3. Work 2 dc at a time on both sides of each dc-groupe.

Rnds 6-7: Work as for rnd 5.

Rnd 8: Net st of ch-7 around, end working "ch 3, 1 tr" instead of ch 7.

Rnd 9: At intervals of 2 arcs, work 2 times of "ch 3, 3-dc puff, ch 3, 1 sc"

Rnd 10: Work as for rnd 9.

Rnd 11: 3 sc, ch 4, repeat.

Rnd 12: Sc in each st around.

Rnd 13: Tr in each st around.

Rnd 14: Repeat rnd 12.

Rnds 15-24: Work dc and ch referring to chart.

Rnds 25-37: Net st of ch-7 between patterns. Make 3-dc puff on rnd 37.

Rnd 38: Work net st of ch-8 around, making "1 3-dc puff, ch 5" at the puff st previous rnd.

Rnd 39: Net st of ch-8 around.

Rnd 40: Net st of ch-9 around.

Rnd 41: Sl st to proceed to the middle of lp, ch 3, 2 dc in same st as ch 3, * ch 2, 3 dc in middle st of next lp, repeat from * around.

Rnd 42: Work sc and ch 4 around.

Rnd 43: 4 sc, ch 4, 4 sc, ch 1, "(1 dc, ch 2) 5 times, 1 dc" in ch-4 lp, ch 1, repeat.

Rnd 44: 3 sc, ch 2, (1 3-dc puff in ch-1 or ch-2, ch 2) 7 times, repeat.

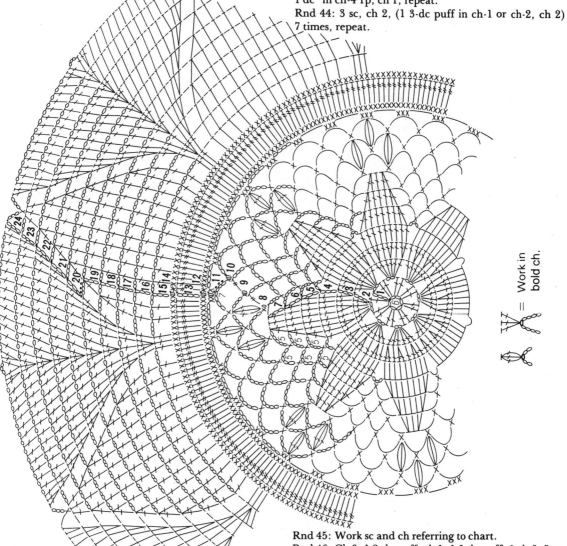

= Work in bold ch.

Rnd 45: Work sc and ch referring to chart.

Rnd 46: Ch 3, 1 2-dc puff, ch 1, 1 3-dc puff, * ch 6, 5 sc in ch-5 lp, ch 6, (1 3-dc puff, ch 1) 3 times, 1 3-dc puff, ch 6, turn the work, sl st in last st of previous ch-6, 6 sc in last ch-6, 1 sl st, repeat from * around. Having worked last ch 1, sl st in 1st puff st, 2 sl st, ch 6, turn, sl st in last st of previous ch-6, 5 sc in last ch-6, sl st in 1st st of 1st ch-6. End off.

55

Center Piece shown on page 18

You'll Need:
D.M.C crochet cotton #20, 4 20-gram balls White.
Steel crochet hook size 0.90 mm.
Finished Size: 52 cm in diameter.
Gauge: 1 row of dc = 0.5 cm.
Making Instructions:
Work in order of ①-⑬.
①: Ch 7. Ch 7, 1 dc in 8th ch from hook, ch 1, sk 1 st, (1 dc, ch 2) 2 times, 1 dc, ch 7, turn (turn each row), (1 dc, ch 1) 3 times, 1 dc, repeat. Work 35 rows in same manner, join to 1st row on 36th row referring to chart.
②: Make center motif. Loop end of cotton.
Row 1: Ch 3, 17 dc in 1p, sl st in 3rd st of beg ch.
Row 2: Ch 4, 2 tr at a time, * ch 4, sl st in 1p of ①, ch 1, sl st in next 1p of ①, ch 4, 3 tr at a time, repeat from * around, end ch 4, sl st in 1st 2 sts at a time.
③: Work 72 rows as for ①.
④: Join cotton in where marked, work ch making sc in the 1p of ①, sl st in the lp of ③.

⑤: Ch 5. Work 168 rows as for ①, joining to ③ with sc and dc.
⑥: Work as for ①, joining to ③ and ⑤.
⑦: Make a motif. Loop end of cotton.
Row 1: Ch 3, 25 dc in 1p, sl st in 3rd st of beg ch.
Row 2: Work 3 dc at a time and ch around, joining to ⑤ and ⑥ as for center motif.
⑧: Ch 9. Work 176 rows as for ①, joining to ⑤ and ⑥.
⑨: Work 308 rows joining to ⑧ as for ⑤.
⑩: Work 308 rows joining to ⑧ and ⑨ as for ⑥.
⑪: Make motif as for ⑦, joining to ⑨ and ⑩.
⑫: Ch 11. Work 264 rows as for ①, joining to ⑨ and ⑩.
⑬: Row 1: Join cotton in the 1p of ⑫, net st of ch-9 around, end working "ch 4, 1 dtr" instead of ch 9.
Row 2: Net st of ch-9 around.
Row 3: Net st of ch-10 around.

Joining Manner (at the end of work):
* Joining last row to 1st row unravelling base ch:
Base ch is worked with another cotton,
last row is worked up to the end of lp.
(Work on wrong side.)

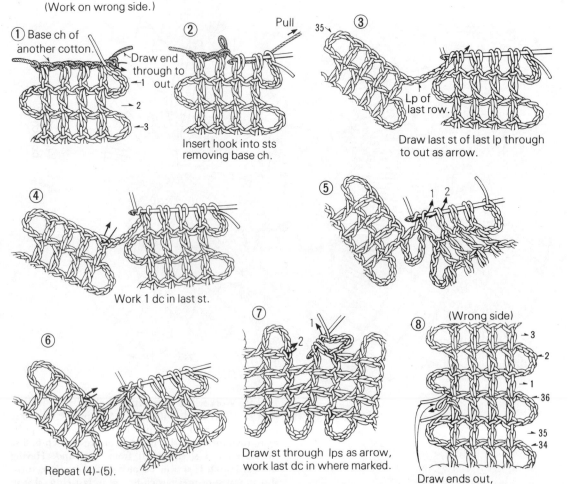

① Base ch of another cotton.
Draw end through to out.

② Pull. Draw end through to out.
Insert hook into sts removing base ch.

③ Lp of last row. Draw last st of last lp through to out as arrow.

④ Work 1 dc in last st.

⑤

⑥ Repeat (4)-(5).

⑦ Draw st through lps as arrow, work last dc in where marked.

⑧ (Wrong side) Draw ends out, tie together, snip off.

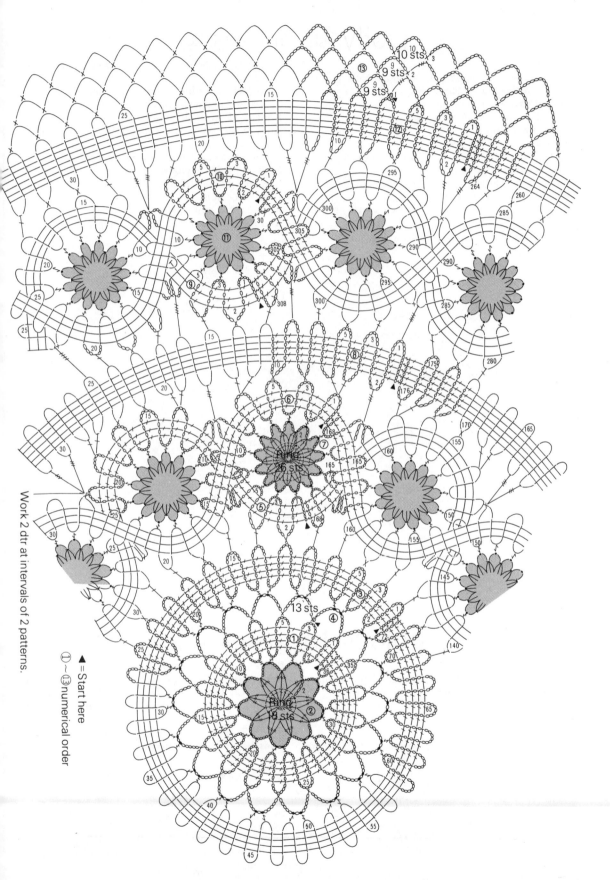

Work 2 dtr at intervals of 2 patterns.

▲ = Start here
① ～ ⑬ numerical order

57

Doily shown on page 20

You'll Need:
D.M.C crochet cotton #20, 11 20-gram balls White.
Steel crochet hook size 0.90 mm.
Finished Size: 95 cm in diameter.
Gauge: 1 row of dc = 0.5 cm.

Making Instructions:
Ch 8, sl st in 1st to form ring.
Rnd 1: Ch 3, 15 dc in ring, sl st in 3rd st of beg ch.
Rnd 2: Alternate 1 dc and ch 2.
Rnd 3: "1 sc, ch 5, 1 sc" in each ch-2 around, end working "ch 2, 1 dc" instead of ch 5.
Rnd 4: 2 dc in ch-5 1p, ch 5, repeat, end working "ch 2, 1 dc" instead of ch 5.
Rnd 5: Net st of ch-6 around, end working "ch 3, 1 dc" instead of ch 6.

Rnd 6: Work shell st ("2 dc, ch 2, 2 dc" in 1p) making ch 3 between.
Rnds 7-21: Referring to chart, make pineapple between shell st, working net st of ch-5 between pineapples.
Rnds 22-31: Work net st following chart.
Rnds 32-65: Work as for rnds 7-31, ending rnd 46 as shown on the chart.
Rnd 66: Join new cotton in, net st of ch-7 around.
Rnds 67-99: Make pineapples working as for rnds 7-20.
Rnd 100: At the fan shape pattern between pineapples, work 1 3-dc puff and ch 5 alternately.
Rnd 101: Net st of ch-6 around.
Rnd 102: 1 sc, ch 3, 1 ch-5 p, ch 3, repeat.

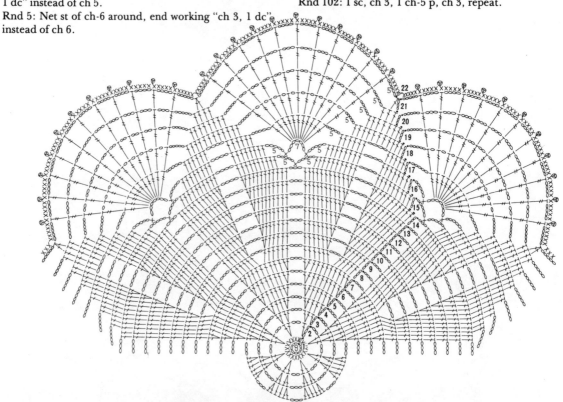

Tablecloth shown on page 19

You'll Need:
D.M.C crochet cotton #5, 3 20-gram balls White.
Steel crochet hook size 1.25 mm.
Finished Size: 32 cm in diameter.
Gauge: 1 row of dc = 0.6 cm.

Making Instructions:
Ch 8, sl st in 1st ch to form ring. Rnd 1: Ch 1, 16 dc in ring, sl st in 1st ch.

Rnd 2: Ch 3, 1 dc in same place as ch 3, (ch 2, sk 1 sc, 2 dc in next sc) 7 times, end ch 2, sl st in 3rd st of beg ch.
Rnd 3: Ch 3, 1 dc in same st as ch 3, 2 dc in next st, (ch 3, 2 dc each in each of 2 dc) 7 times, ch 3, sl st in 3rd st of beg ch.
Rnds 4-7: Work as for rnd 3, increasing side st of dc.
Rnds 8-14: Dc and ch referring to chart.

Way of the Sts:

Having worked ch 1, make a incomplete of tr.

Make a incomplete of dc, insert hook as arrow, draw lp through to out.

Draw through as arrow 3 times.

Rnd 15: Work as for previous rnds, making "ch 5, 1 sc, ch 5" at the 1p between patterns.
Rnd 16: Work as for previous rnd.
Rnd 17: 11 tr in ch-7 1p.

Rnds 18-21: Referring to chart, work ch and tr to form fan shape patterns.
Rnd 22: 5 sc in ch-5 1p, 1 sc in tr, 1 ch-3 p, repeat.

(Continued next page)

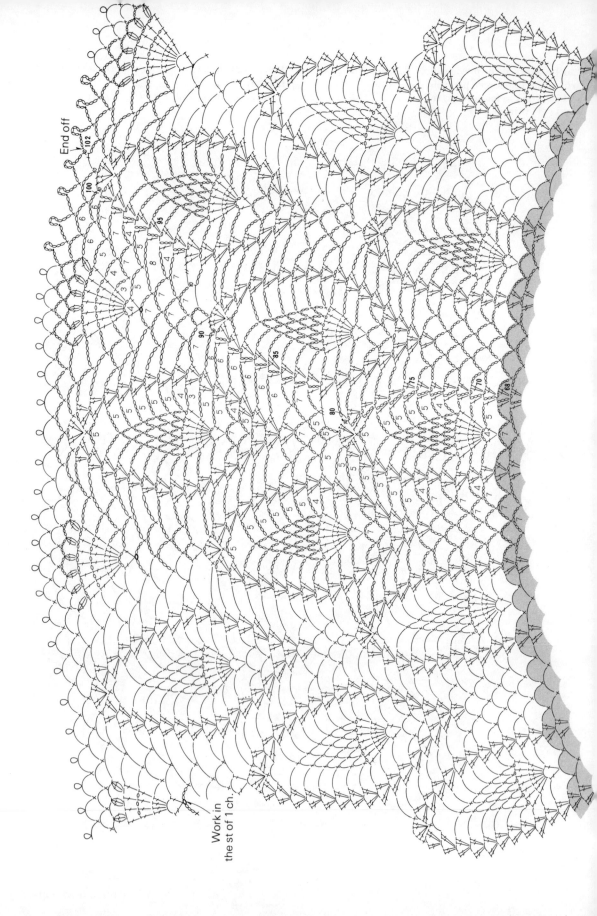

End off

Work in
the st of 1 ch.

60

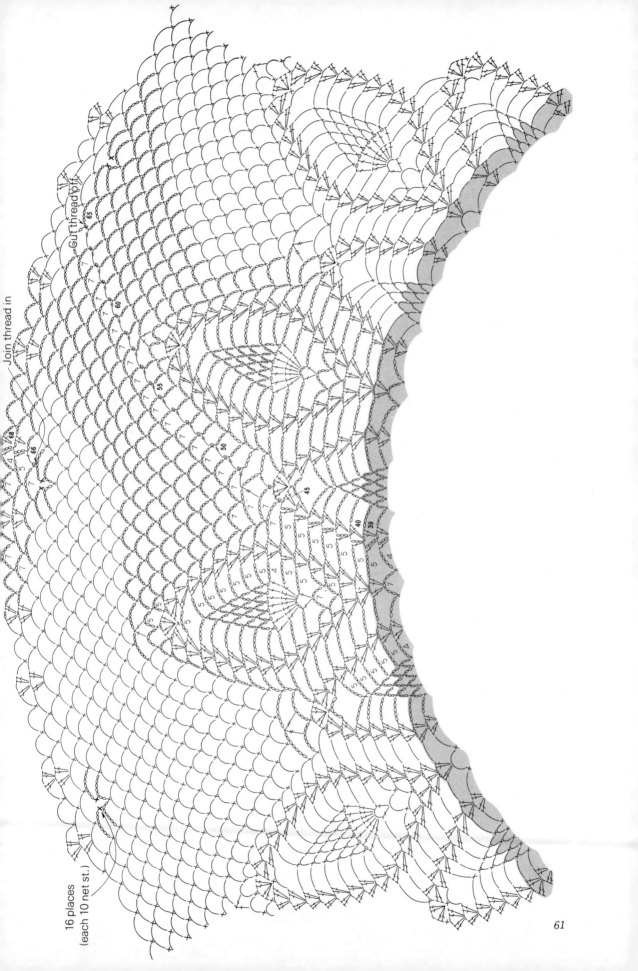

Cut Thread off

Join thread in

16 places
(each 10 net st.)

61

Doily shown on page 21

You'll Need:
D.M.C crochet cotton #20, 2 20-gram balls White.
Steel crochet hook size 0.90 mm.
Finished Size: 30 cm in diameter.
Gauge: 1 row of dc = 0.5 cm.
Making Instructions:
Ch 10, sl st in 1st ch to form ring. Rnd 1: Ch 3, 23 dc in ring, sl st in 3rd st of beg ch.
Rnd 2: Ch 3, 1 dc in next st, (ch 3, sk 1 dc, 2 dc) 7 times, end ch 3, sl st in 3rd st of beg ch.
Rnd 3: 2 sl st, ch 3, 4 dc in lp, * ch 2, 5 dc in next lp, repeat from * around, end ch 2, sl st in 3rd st of beg ch.
Rnd 4: Work as for rnd 3, making 2 dc each in side st of dc.

Rnds 5-7: Work dc and ch as for previous rnds.
Rnds 8-13: Make a pattern of tr between the patterns of dc, working ch and sc between tr and dc. End 12th and 13th rnd making "ch 3, 1 tr".
Rnds 14-19: Make new pattern working 1 dc and ch 1. As for the dc on 14th rnd, work each in bold ch referring to chart.
Rnd 20: Work as for rnd 19: end making 1 dtr in 3rd st of beg ch.
Rnds 21-24: Work as for previous rnds. From rnd 22, work net st making "1 sc, ch 3, 1 sc" in each lp around. End last rnd working "ch 4, 1 dtr" instead of ch 9
Rnds 25-26: 1 sc, ch 3, 1 sc, ch 9, repeat.
Rnd 27: 1 sc, ch 3, 1 sc, ch 10, repeat.

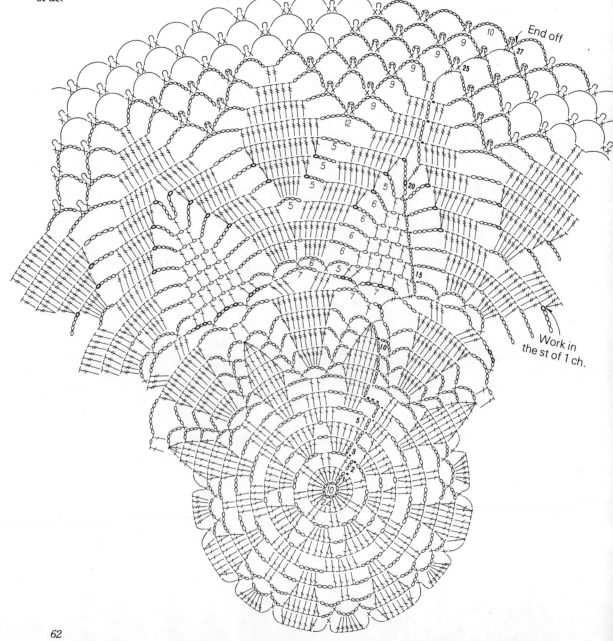

End off

Work in the st of 1 ch.

Doily shown on page 23

You'll Need:

D.M.C crochet cotton #15, 3 20-gram balls White.
Steel crochet hook size 1.00 mm.

Finished Size: 37 cm in diameter.

Gauge: 1 row of tr = 0.9 cm.

Size of Motif: 5 cm in diameter.

Making Instructions:

Loop end of cotton. Rnd 1: Ch 3, 1 dc in 1p, (ch 2, 2 dc) 5 times in 1p, ch 2, sl st in 3rd st of beg ch.

Rnd 2: 2 sl st, ch 4, 4 tr in 1p, ch 3, * 5 tr in next lp, ch 3, repeat from * around, sl st in 4th st of beg ch.

Rnd 3: Ch 4, 4 tr at a time, 1 ch-4 p, * ch 4, 1 sc in 1p, ch 7, 1 sc in same 1p as sc, ch 4, 5 tr at a time, 1 ch-4 p, repeat from * around.

Rnds 4-13: Work as for rnds 2-3.

Motif: Work rnds 1-3. Make 12 pieces.

Edging: Rnd 1: Join cotton in motif, work as for rnd 2 of center motif.

Rnd 2: Work as for rnd 3 of center motif.

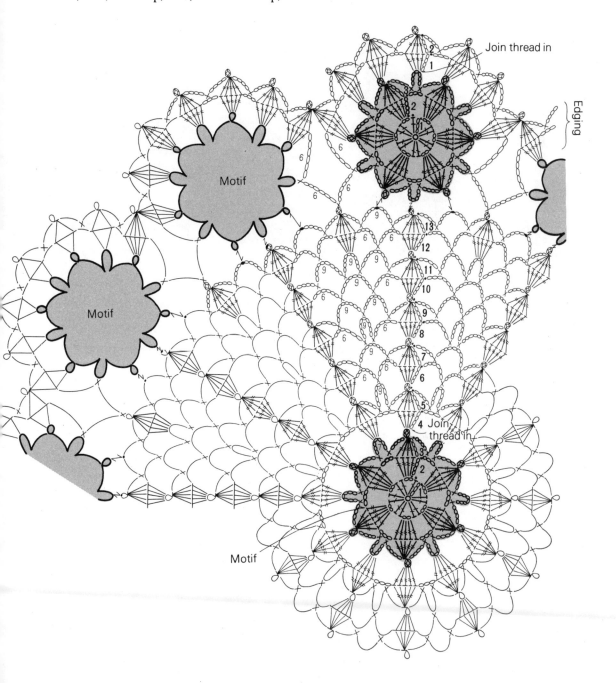

Doily shown on page 24 above

You'll Need:
D.M.C crochet cotton #20, 1 20-gram ball White. Steel crochet hook size 0.90 mm.
Finished Size: 24 cm in diameter.
Gauge: 1 row of tr = 0.7 cm.
Making Instructions:
Ch 8, sl st in 1st ch to form ring. Rnd 1: Ch 4, 2 tr in ring, (ch 3, 3 tr) 7 times, end ch 3, sl st in 4th st of beg ch.
Rnd 2: Work as for rnd 1, making "ch 2, 1 dc, ch 2" in middle st of ch-3.

Rnds 3-4: Work as for rnd 2, making 2 tr each in side st of 3 tr.
Rnds 5-13: Work pineapple pattern in 8 places referring to chart.
Rnd 14: Alternate 1 2 tr puff and ch 3 at the ch-1 between pineapples.
Rnd 15: Work as for rnd 14.
Rnd 16: 2 sl st, ch 4, 1 tr in next st, ch 9, * (1 2-tr puff in ch-5, ch 6, 1 ch-2 p, ch 5) 5 times, 1 2-tr puff, ch 9, 2 tr at a time, repeat from * around.

End off

Work in the st of 1 ch.

Doily shown on page 22

You'll Need:

D.M.C crochet cotton #20, 2.5 20-gram balls White.
Steel crochet hook size 1.00 mm.

Finished Size: 44 cm in diameter.

Gauge: 1 row of tr = 0.7 cm.

Making Instructions:

Loop end of cotton. Rnd 1: Ch 3 to form 1st st, ch 5, (1 dc in 1p, ch 5) 5 times, sl st in 3rd st of beg ch.

Rnd 2: Ch 3 to form 1st st, ch 4, *1 dc in 1p, ch 4, 1 dc in next 1p, ch 4, repeat from * around, end ch 4, sl st in 3rd st of beg ch.

Rnd 3: Ch 3 to form 1st st, ch 4, * 3 sc in ch and dc, ch 4, 1 dc in dc, ch 4, repeat from * around.

Rnd 4: Ch 2, 1 hdc in 1p, ch 2, 1 tr and 2 tr in same 1p as hdc, 1 tr each in 3 sc, 2 tr in next 1p, 2 sts (1 tr and upside down of Y-st) at a time in same 1p as last 2 tr and next dc, ch 9, continue in same manner.

Rnds 5-6: Work as for rnd 4, making new pattern between petals. Refer to chart for the variation of Y-st.

Rnds 7-16: Work same way referring to chart.

Rnd 17: Proceed ch-8 1p with sl st, ch 4, 1 ud (upside down) Y-st, ch 11, 2 sts (tr and ud Y-st) at a time, ch 11, continue in same way referring to chart.

Rnd 18: Work net st of ch-11 around.

Rnd 19: Net st of ch-11, working "(1 tr, ch 1) 6 times, 1 tr" in middle 1p between patterns.

Rnds 20-24: Work as for previous rnds, making "1 Y-st, ch 7, 1 Y-st" at the place where indicated on the chart.

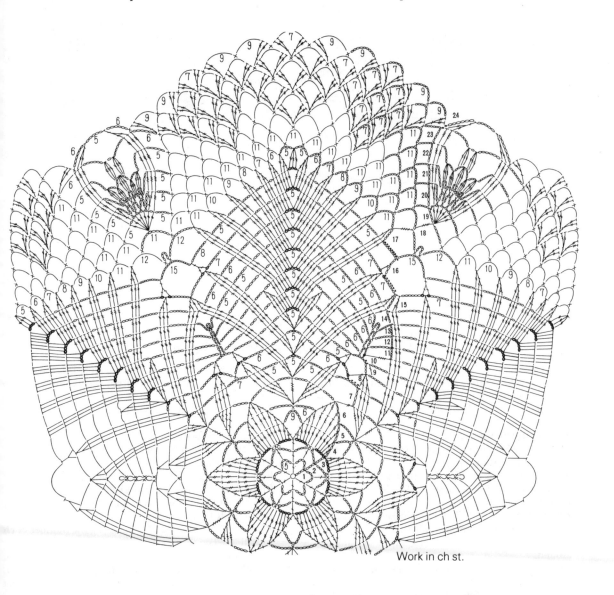

Work in ch st.

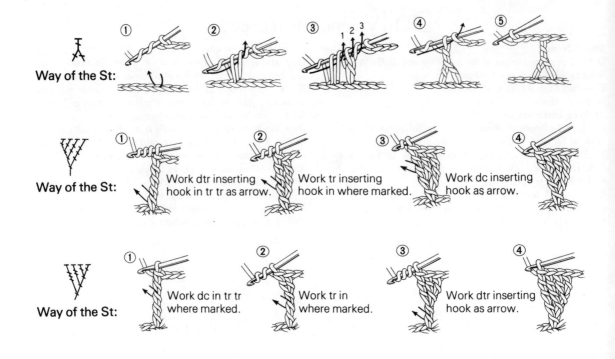

Way of the St:

① ② ③ ④ ⑤

Way of the St:

① Work dtr inserting hook in tr tr as arrow. ② Work tr inserting hook in where marked. ③ Work dc inserting hook as arrow. ④

Way of the St:

① Work dc in tr tr where marked. ② Work tr in where marked. ③ Work dtr inserting hook as arrow. ④

Doily shown on page 24 below

You'll Need:
D.M.C crochet cotton #20, 1.5 20-gram balls White. Steel crochet hook size 1.00 mm.
Finished Size: 37 cm in diameter.
Gauge: 1 row of dc = 0.6 cm.
Making Instructions:
Ch 8, sl t in 1st ch to form ring. Rnd 1: Ch 3, 19 dc in ring, sl st in 3rd st of beg ch.
Rnd 2: Ch 1, 1 sc, (ch 5, sk 1 st, 1 sc in dc) 9 times, end working "ch 2, 1 dc" instead of ch 5.
Rnd 3: Net st of ch-7.
Rnd 4: 1 sc, (ch 3, 1 ch-4 p) 2 times, ch 7, 1 ch-4 p, ch 3, 1 ch-4 p, ch 3, repeat. End off.
Rnd 5: Join new cotton in, alternate 1 sc and ch 15 around.
Rnd 6: Ch 3 to form 1st st, ch 1, * sk 1 st, 1 dc in next st, ch 1, repeat from * around.
Rnds 7-9: Work as for rnd 6, making ch 2 instead of ch 1. Make 2 dc instead of ch 2 at intervals of 3 squares on rnd 7.

Rnd 10: Ch 1, 1 ch-4 p, ch 1, "1 dc, ch 3, 1 dc" in ch-2 p, ch 1, 1 ch-4 p, ch 1, repeat from top at intervals of 5 sps.
Rnd 11: In ch-3 1p, work ch 4, (1 dc, ch 1) 5 times, 1 dc, ch 4.
Rnds 12-16: Work as for rnds 7-9.
Rnd 21: Ch 3, (ch 3, 1 sc, ch 3, 1 dc) 2 times, 10 dc, (ch 3, 1 sc, ch 3, 1 dc) 5 times, repeat.
Rnd 22: Alternate 1 dc and ch 6 around.
Rnds 23-24: Work as for rnds 21-22 referring to chart.
Rnd 25: At ch-11, work ch 4, 1 ch-4 p, ch 4, 2 sc, ch 4, 1 ch-4 p, ch 4.
Rnd 26: Work as for rnd 24, following the number of ch sts indicated on the chart.
Rnd 27: Proceed 4 sts working sl st, (1 sc, ch 4, 1 ch-4 p, ch 4) 3 times, 1 sc, ch 7, (1 2-tr tr puff, ch 4, 1 ch-4 p, ch 4) 4 times and 1 2-tr tr puff in ch-5 lp, ch 7. Repeat in same way around.

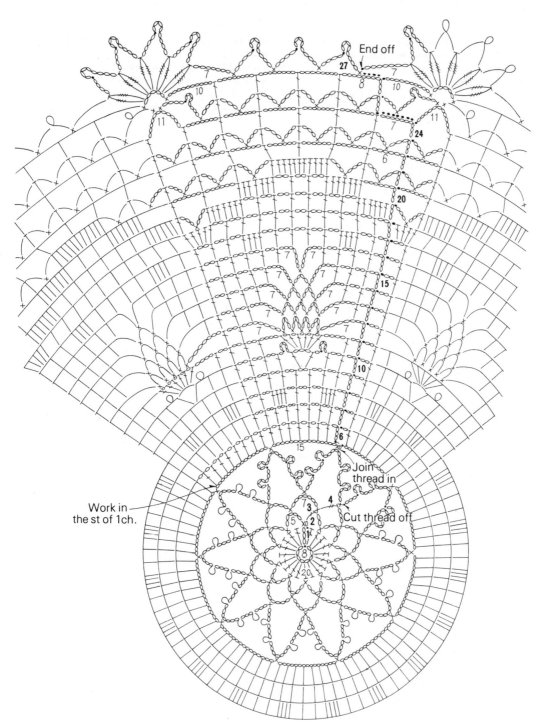

Doily shown on page 25

You'll Need:
D.M.C crochet cotton #20, 1.5 20-gram balls White.
Steel crochet hook size 0.90 mm.
Finished Size: 31 cm in diameter.
Gauge: 1 row of dc = 0.6 cm.

Making Instructions:

Loop end of cotton. Rnd 1: Ch 3, 15 dc in lp, sl st in 3rd st of beg ch.

Rnd 2: Ch 5 to form 1st st, ch 3, (1 dtr, ch 3) 15 times, sl st in 5th st of beg ch.

Rnd 3: Ch 1, 1 sc, * "2 sc, 1 ch-3 p, 1 sc" in ch-3 1p, 1 sc in next dtr, repeat from * around, sl st in beg ch.

Rnd 4: Alternate 1 dc and ch 5 around.

Rnd 5: Dc in each st around, making ch-3 p at every 8th dc.

Rnd 6: Ch 1, 1 sc, 1 sc in next dc, * ch 13, sk 5 dc, 3 sc, repeat from * around, end working "ch 7, 1 tr tr" instead of ch 13.

Rnd 7: 13 sc in lp, 1 sc in sc, repeat.

Rnd 8: 1 sc, * (ch 3, 1 tr) 5 times, ch 3, 3 sc, repeat from * around, sl st in 1st st.

Rnd 9: Work as for rnd 3.

Rnd 10: Alternate 3 arcs of ch-9 net and 1 arc of ch-13 net.

Rnd 11: Net st of ch-10, working "3 dc, 1 ch-3 p, 2 dc" in ch-13 1p.

Rnds 12-15: Work as for rnds 10-11.

Rnds 16-22: Work as for rnds 6-9.

Rnd 23: Alternate sc and p, working (ch 3, 2 dc in same st, ch 3, 1 sl st) 2 times at the middle of each arc.

Doily shown on page 26

You'll Need:
D.M.C crochet cotton #20, 2 20-gram balls White.
Steel crochet hook size 0.90 mm.
Finished Size: 32 cm in diameter.
Gauge: 1 row of dc = 0.6 cm.
Making Instructions:
Ch 8, sl st in 1st ch to form ring.
Rnd 1: Ch 3, 19 dc in ring, sl st in 3rd st of beg ch.
Rnd 2: Ch 1, 1 sc, (ch 5, sk 1 st, 1 sc) 9 times, end working "ch 2, 1 hdc" instead of ch 5.
Rnd 3: Alternate 1 dc and ch 5.
Rnd 4: Ch 1, 7 dc in each 1p around.
Rnd 5: Net st of ch-4, skipping 2 sts (1 st for the 1st arc) each for each arc.
Rnd 6: Ch 3 to form 1st st, ch 3, 1 dc, ch 5, sk 1 1p, "1 dc, ch 3, 1 dc" in next 1p, ch 5, repeat, end sl st in

3rd st of beg ch.
Rnd 7: 2 sl st, ch 3, "1 dc, ch 2, 2 dc" in 1p, * ch 6, "2 dc, ch 2, 2 dc" (shell st) in next 1p, repeat from * around.
Rnd 8: Work as for rnd 7.
Rnd 9: Ch 5, 1 sc, ch 5 between shell sts.
Rnd 10: Work as for rnd 9.
Rnd 11: 9 dc in ch-2 of shell st. Ch 6, 2 dc at a time, ch 6 between shell sts.
Rnd 12: Alternate 1 dc and ch 1, working ch 7 between patterns.
Rnd 13: Work as for rnd 12.
Rnds 14-21: Make pineapples working 4-dc puff referring to chart.
Rnds 22-25: Shell st referring to chart. On rnd 25th, work "3 dc, 1 ch-3 p, 2 dc" every 2nd shell st.

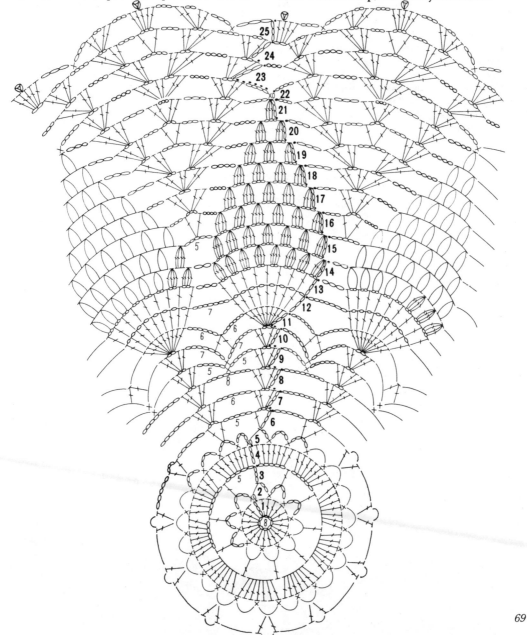

Tablecloth shown on page 27

You'll Need:
D.M.C crochet cotton #20, 15.5 20-gram balls White.
Steel crochet hook size 0.80 mm.
Finished Size: Refer to chart.
Gauge: 1 row of dc = 0.6 cm.
Size of Motif: Refer to chart.
Making Instructions:
Motif: Loop end of cotton. Rnd 1: Ch 3,
1 dc in 1p, (ch 2, 1 2-dc puff) 11 times in 1p,
ch 2, sl st in 1st ch.
Rnd 2: Ch 4, 1 3-tr puff in ch-2, * ch 5,
1 sc in next 1p, ch 5, 1 4-tr puff, repeat
from * around.
Rnd 3: Ch 4, 1 tr in same st as ch 4, ch 3,
3 tr in same st as tr, ch 3, 1 dc in sc, 1 ch-3 p,
ch 3, sc in puff st, ch 3, 1 dc in sc, 1 ch-3 p,
ch 3, 3 tr in next puff st, ch 3, 2 tr in same
puff st, continue in same way around.
Rnds 4-5: Work as for rnd 3, making 5 times
of "1 3-tr puff, 1 ch-3 p" at the corner on rnd 5.
From 2nd motif, work last rnd joining to
adjacent side, Make 150 motifs.
Fill-in Motif: Loop at end of cotton. Rnd 1:
Ch 3, 1 dc in 1p, * ch 1, 1 ch-3 p, ch 1, 2-dc
puff, ch 6, join to motif, ch 5, 1 2-dc puff,
repeat from * around.

Chart of measurements (Joining motifs)

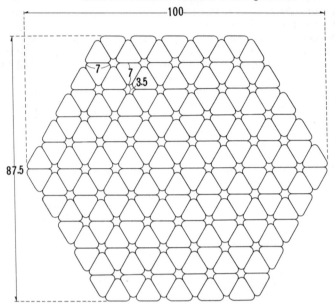

Motif, the way of joining

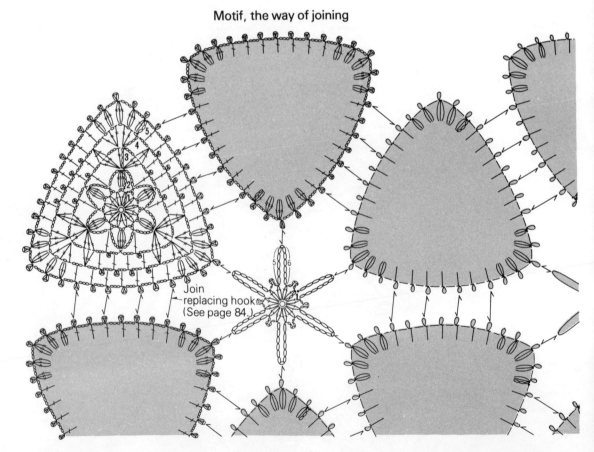

Join
replacing hook
(See page 84.)

Tablecloth shown on page 31

You'll Need:

D.M.C crochet cotton #20, 22 20-gram balls White.
Steel crochet hook size 1.00 mm.

Finished Size: 129.5 cm by 99.5 cm.

Gauge: 1 row of dc = 0.6 cm.

Size of Motif: 7.5 cm square.

Making Instructions:

A-Motif: Ch 8, sl st in 1st ch to form ring.

Rnd 1: Ch 1, (1 sc in ring, ch 7) 7 times, 1 sc in ring, end working "ch 4, 1 dc" instead of ch 7.

Rnd 2: Ch 3, 1 3-dc puff in 1p, * ch 7, 1 sc in next 1p, ch 7, "1 4-dc puff, ch 7, 1 4-dc puff" in next 1p, repeat from * around, end 4-dc puff in last 1p, "ch 4, 1 dc" instead of ch 7.

Rnds 3-6: Work as for rnd 2.

B-Motif: Ch 6, sl st in 1st ch to form ring.

Rnd 1: Ch 3, 15 dc in ring, sl st in 3rd st of beg ch.

Rnd 2: Ch 3 to form last st, ch 2, (1 dc in dc, ch 2) 15 times, sl st in 3rd st of beg ch.

Rnd 3: 3 dc in ch-2 1p, ch 2, 3 dc in next ch-2 1p, ch 1, repeat.

Rnd 4: Ch 1, * 4 sc, ch 13, 5 sc, 1 ch-4 p, repeat from * around.

Rnd 5: Proceed 6 sts working sl st, ch 3, 14 dc in 1p, * 15 dc in next 1p, repeat from * around.

Rnd 6: Net st of ch-7 (ch-9 at the corner referring to chart), end working "ch 3, 1 tr" instead of ch 7.

Rnd 7: Work net st (1 4-dc puff, ch 9, 1 4-dc puff at the corner), making sl st in A-motif as shown.

Referring to chart, join motifs A and B alternately.

Make 13 rows of 17 motifs.

Edging: Rnd 1: Net st of ch-7 (ch-9 at the corner) around.

Rnd 2: 10 dc in 1p, making 12 dc in corner 1p.

Chart of measurements
A---111 pieces
B---110 pieces

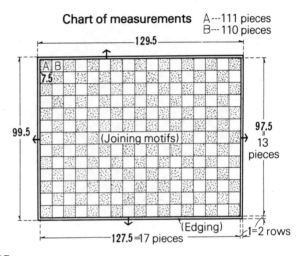

Motif, the way to joining, edging

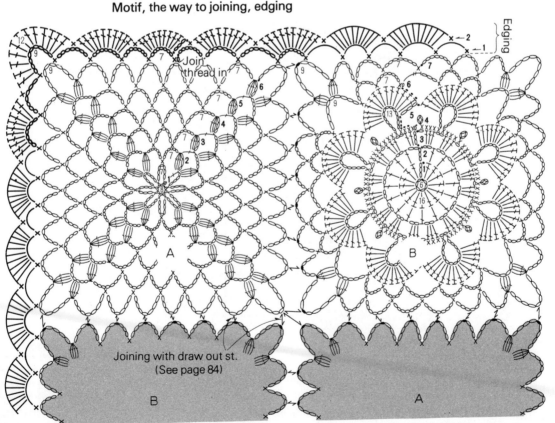

Joining with draw out st.
(See page 84)

71

Tablecloth shown on page 30

You'll Need:
D.M.C crochet cotton #5, 62 20-gram balls White.
Steel crochet hook size 1.50 mm.
Finished Size: 133 cm square.
Gauge: (Filet crochet) Motifs A, B, D, E; 15 squares =

10 cm, 16 rows = 10 cm. Motif C; 16 squares = 10 cm, 16 rows = 10 cm.
Making Instructions:
A-Motif: Ch 28. Row 1: Ch 4 to form 1st st, ch 2, 4 dc starting at 7th ch from hook, (ch 2, sk 2 ch, 4 dc)

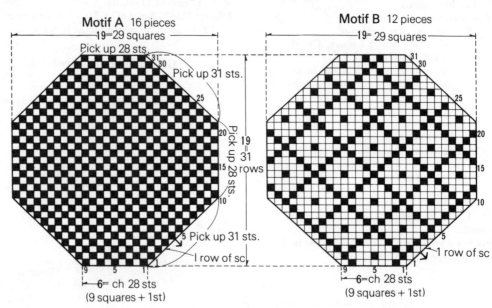

Motif A 16 pieces
19 = 29 squares
Pick up 28 sts.
Pick up 31 sts.
Pick up 28 sts.
19 = 31 rows
Pick up 31 sts.
1 row of sc
6 = ch 28 sts
(9 squares + 1st)

Motif B 12 pieces
19 = 29 squares
1 row of sc
6 = ch 28 sts
(9 squares + 1st)

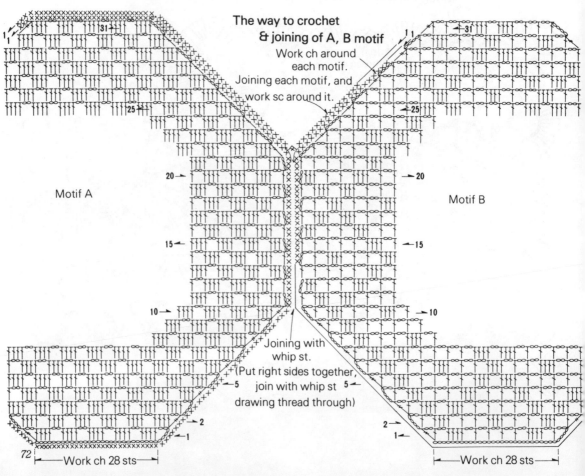

**The way to crochet
& joining of A, B motif**
Work ch around each motif.
Joining each motif, and work sc around it.

Motif A

Motif B

Joining with whip st.
(Put right sides together, join with whip st drawing thread through)

72 ⊢ Work ch 28 sts ⊣

⊢ Work ch 28 sts ⊣

4 times, ch 2, 1 tr in same st as last dc.

Row 2: Turn (turn each row), work as for row 1, wrapping ch 2 in 2 dc.

Rows 3-10: Work as for row 2, increasing each side.

Rows 11-21: Work straight.

Rows 22-31: Work decreasing each side. Begin each row making ch 4, end making 2 sts (dc and tr) at a time.

Work 1 row of sc around. Make 16 motifs in same manner.

B-Motif: Ch 28, work as for A. Make 1 row of sc around. Crochet 12 motifs in same manner.

C-Motif: Ch 31. Row 1: Ch 4 to form 1st st, ch 2, 1 dc in 7th ch from hook, * ch 3, sk 2 ch, 1 sc, ch 3, sk 2 ch, 1 dc, repeat from * across, end ch 2, 1 tr in same st as last dc.

Row 2: Ch 4 to form 1st st, ch 5, 1 dc in dc, * ch 5, 1 dc in next dc, repeat from * across, end ch 5, 1 tr in 4th st of beg ch.

Rows 3-10: Work as for rows 1-2, increasing each side.

Rows 11-21: Work straight.

Rows 22-31: Work decreasing each side.

Row 32: Alternate 1 sc and ch 5.

Make 1 row of sc around. Crochet 12 motifs.

D-Motif: Ch 28. Row 1: Ch 4 to form 1st st, ch 2, 1 dc each in each of 28 sts, starting at 7th ch from hook, ch 2, tr in same st as last dc.

Rows 2-3: Work as for C-motif.

Rows 4-10: Work increasing each side.

Rows 11-21: Work straight.

Rows 22-31: Work decreasing each side.

Make 1 row of sc around. Crochet 9 motifs in same way.

E-Motif: Ch 1. Rows 1-10: Alternate 1 dc and ch 2, increasing each side.

Rows 11-20: Work decreasing each side.

Make 1 row of sc around. Crochet 36 motifs in same way.

Joining: Join each motif together with whip stitch referring to chart.

Edging: Work 1 row of sc around.

Chart of measurements

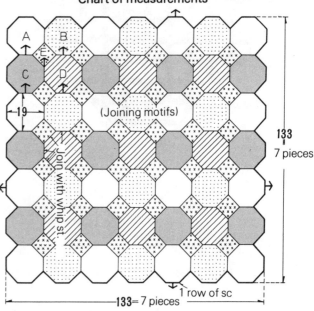

(Joining motifs)

133 = 7 pieces

133 = 7 pieces

1 row of sc

Motif C 12 pieces

19 = 30 squares

Pick up 28 sts.

Pick up 31 sts.

Pick up 28 sts.

Pick up 31 sts.

19 / 32 rows

1 row of sc

6 = ch 31 sts
(10 squares + 1st)

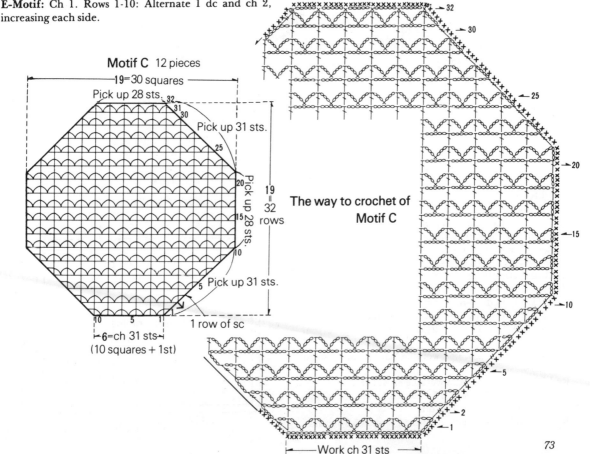

The way to crochet of Motif C

Work ch 31 sts

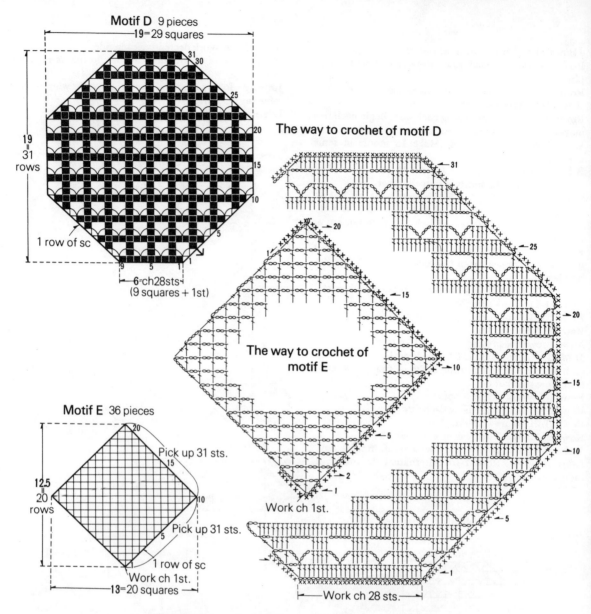

Motif D 9 pieces
19=29 squares

19 = 31 rows

1 row of sc

The way to crochet of motif D

6 ch 28 sts
(9 squares + 1st)

31 30
25
20
15
10
5
9 5 1

The way to crochet of motif E

Work ch 1st.

Motif E 36 pieces

Pick up 31 sts.
Pick up 31 sts.

12.5
20 rows

1 row of sc
Work ch 1st.

13=20 squares

Work ch 28 sts.

Tablecloth shown on page 28

You'll Need:
D.M.C crochet cotton #20, 21 20-gram balls White.
Steel crochet hook size 0.75 mm.
Finished Size: 124 cm by 98 cm.
Gauge: 1 row of dc = 0.6 cm.
Size of Motif: 13 cm squares
Making Instructions:
Motif: Ch 10, sl st in 1st ch to form ring.
Rnd 1: Ch 1, 16 dc in ring, sl st in 1st ch.
Rnd 2: Ch 1, 1 sc, (ch 3, sk 1 st, 1 sc) 8 times.
Rnd 3: Ch 4, 5 tr, 1 pop, * ch 7, 1 6-tr pop, repeat from * around.
Rnd 4: Net st of ch-5, end working "ch 2, 1 dc" instead of ch 5.
Rnd 5: Net st of ch-7, end working ch 3, 1 tr.
Rnd 6: "1 sc, ch 5, 1 sc, ch 7, 1 sc, ch 5, 1 sc" in middle st of ch-7, ch 5, repeat. End off.
Rnd 7: Join new cotton in, alternate 1 sc and ch 9 around.

Chart of measurements

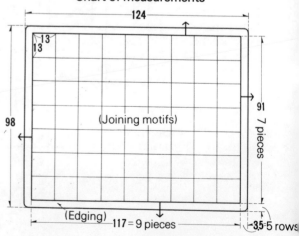

124

13
13

(Joining motifs)

98

91

7 pieces

(Edging) 117 = 9 pieces

3.5 = 5 rows

Rnd 8: 11 sc in each 1p around.

Rnd 9: 2 sl st, ch 3, 2 dc, ch 3, sk 3 sts, 1 sc, (ch 5, 1 sc) 4 times, ch 3, sk 3 sts, 3 dc, ch 5, (1 dc, ch 1) 4 times, 1 dc, ch 5, 3 dc, repeat in same way around.

Rnds 10-14: Work as for rnd 9.

Rnd 15: Ch 4, 2 tr at a time, 3 tr at a time, sl at in previous st, ch 4, 1 tr between sts, 1 ch-7 p, ch 4 1 sl st in 3 sts at a time, ch 9, 1 sc in ch-5 1p, (ch 3, 1 sc) 16 times, ch 9, 2 times of 3 tr at a time, continue in same way around.

From 2nd motif, work rnd 15 making sc in adjacent motif. Make 7 rows of 9 motifs.

Border: Rnd 1: Join new cotton in, alternate 1 dc and ch 3, making "1 dc, ch 3, 1 dc" at corners and between motifs.

Rnd 2: Net st of ch-7, end working "ch 3, 1 tr" instead of ch 7.

Rnds 3-4: Work as for rnd 2.

Rnd 5: Ch 3, 1 dc in 1p, * ch 5, 4 dc in next 1p, repeat from * around, making "4 dc, ch 5, 4 dc" in corner 1p.

Motif, the way to joining, edging

Work in previous row's center st.

Bedspread shown on page 32

You'll Need:
D.M.C crochet cotton #5, 149 20-gram balls Beige.
Steel crochet hook size 1.60 mm.
Finished Size: 273 cm by 186 cm.
Gauge: 1 row of dc = 0.7 cm.
Size of Motif: 29 cm square.
Making Instructions:
Motif: Ch 10, sl st in 1st ch to form ring.

Rnd 1: Ch 3, 23 dc in ring, sl st in 3rd st of beg ch.
Rnd 2: Work 2 dc at a time and ch 3 alternately around.
Rnd 3: 4 dc in ch-3 1p, 1 dc in the st of 2 dc at a time.
Rnd 4: Alternate 3 dc at a time and ch 7 around.
Rnd 5: 7 dc in ch-7 1p, 1 dc in the st of 3 dc at a time.
Rnd 6: Sc in each st around.
Rnd 7: Ch 3, 2 dc in next st, * ch 2, sk 2 sts, 1 sc, (ch 5, sk 3 sts, 1 sc) 4 times, ch 2, sk 2 sts, 2 dc in next

75

Motif, the way to joining, edging

Cut thread off

Join thread in

(Edging)

76

st, 1 dc in next st, ch 3, 1 dc, 2 dc in next st, repeat from * around, end working "ch 1, 1 hdc" instead of ch 3.

Rnds 8-25: Work as for rnd 7, increasing sts at the corner. Make 4 dc in net st referring to chart.

Rnd 26: Net st of ch-6 around.

From 2nd motif, work rnd 26 making sl st in previous motif to join. Make 9 rows of 6 motifs.

Border: Rnd 1: Join cotton in, ch 3, 2 dc in 1p, * ch 2, 1 sc in next 1p, ch 2, 3 dc in next 1p, ch 3, 3 dc in same 1p as last 3 dc, repeat from * around, making "1 sc, ch 2, 1 sc" at the corner.

Rnds 2-6: Work as for rnd 1.

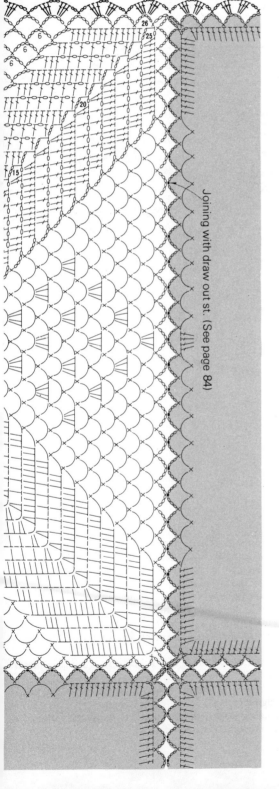

Joining with draw out st (See page 84)

Chart of measurements

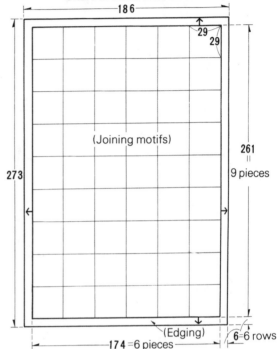

186

29
29

273

(Joining motifs)

261
=
9 pieces

(Edging)

6=6 rows

174 =6 pieces

Tablecloth shown on page 29

You'll Need:
D.M.C crochet cotton #20, 20 20-gram balls White. Steel crochet hook size 0.90 mm. Light weight White linen 90 cm square. 6-strand embroidery floss 2 skeins White.

Finished Size: 152.5 cm by 121.5 cm.

Gauge: 1 row of dc = 0.5 cm.

Size of Motif: 4.5 cm in diameter.

Making Instructions:

Motif: Ch 6, sl st in 1st ch to form ring.

Rnd 1: Ch 3, 15 dc in ring, sl st in 3rd st of beg ch.

Rnd 2: Ch 3 to form 1st st, ch 2, * 1 dc in dc, ch 2, repeat from * around, sl st in 3rd st of beg ch.

Rnd 3: 1 3-dc puff in ch-2, ch 5, repeat, end working "ch 2, 1 dc" instead of ch 5.

Rnd 4: Alternate 1 sc and ch 5.

From 2nd motif, work rnd 4 joining to adjacent motif. Make 3 rows of 3 motifs.

Fill-in Motif: Join cotton in motif, ch 4, 1 2-tr puff, (ch 1, 1 3-tr puff in middle st of next 1p) 7 times, ch 1, sl st in 1st puff st. End off. Fill 4 sps in same manner.

Edging-(1): Row 1: Join cotton in motif, 1 sc, ch 5, 1 sc in next 1p, ch 5, 1 dc in next 1p, ch 5, 2 tr at a time in next 1p and the 1p after next, ch 5, continue in same way around.

Row 2: Alternate 1 dc and ch 5, making "1 tr, ch 7, 1 tr" in corner 1p. Finish 32 pieces in same manner.

Fabric Motif: Cut 31 pieces of 15 cm square in size out from linen, embroider middle of each, fold back 2.5 mm all around, work edging-(2) along.

Motif, the way to joining, edging

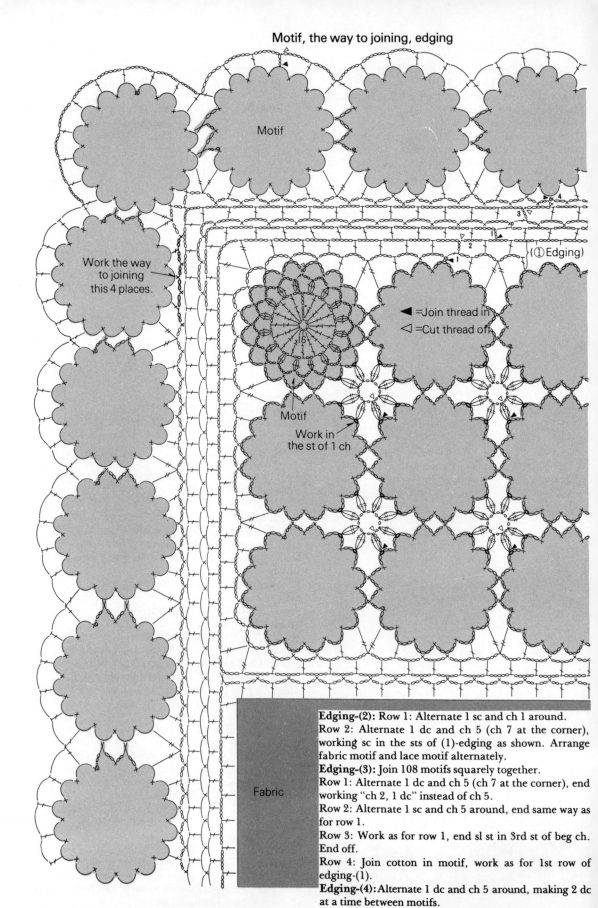

Motif

Work the way to joining this 4 places.

Motif

Work in the st of 1 ch

Motif

(①Edging)

◄ =Join thread in
◁ =Cut thread off

Fabric

Edging-(2): Row 1: Alternate 1 sc and ch 1 around.
Row 2: Alternate 1 dc and ch 5 (ch 7 at the corner), working sc in the sts of (1)-edging as shown. Arrange fabric motif and lace motif alternately.
Edging-(3): Join 108 motifs squarely together.
Row 1: Alternate 1 dc and ch 5 (ch 7 at the corner), end working "ch 2, 1 dc" instead of ch 5.
Row 2: Alternate 1 sc and ch 5 around, end same way as for row 1.
Row 3: Work as for row 1, end sl st in 3rd st of beg ch. End off.
Row 4: Join cotton in motif, work as for 1st row of edging-(1).
Edging-(4): Alternate 1 dc and ch 5 around, making 2 dc at a time between motifs.

78

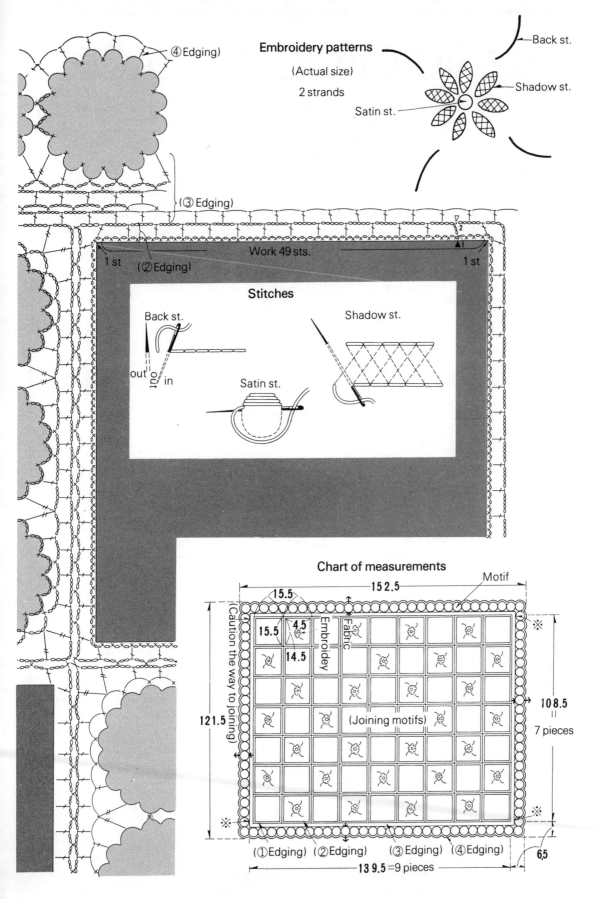

④Edging)

Embroidery patterns

(Actual size)

2 strands

Back st.

Shadow st.

Satin st.

(③ Edging)

1 st (②Edging)

Work 49 sts. 1 st

2

Stitches

Back st.

out out in

Shadow st.

Satin st.

Chart of measurements

Motif

15 2.5

15.5

15.5 4.5

(Caution the way to joining)

15.5 14.5

Embroidery

Fabric

121.5

(Joining motifs)

108.5
=
7 pieces

※

※

※

(①Edging) (②Edging)   (③ Edging) (④Edging)

6.5

13 9.5 =9 pieces

BASIC CROCHET LACE

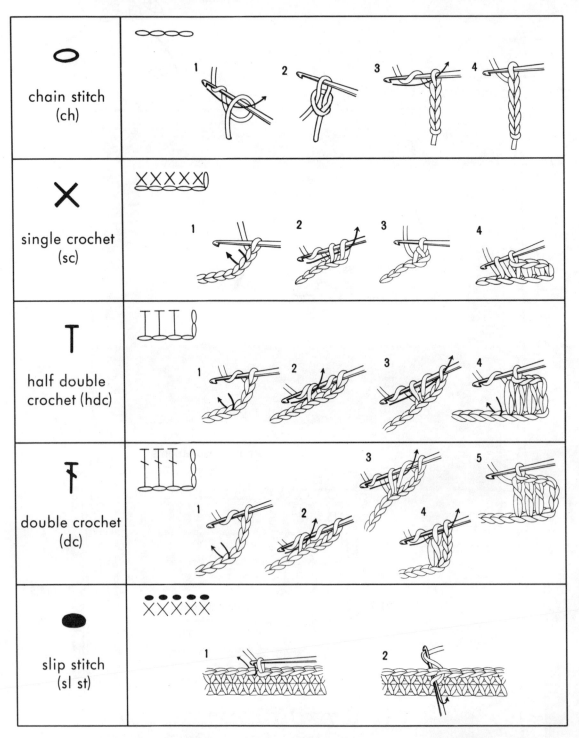

O chain stitch (ch)	
X single crochet (sc)	
T half double crochet (hdc)	
⊤ double crochet (dc)	
● slip stitch (sl st)	

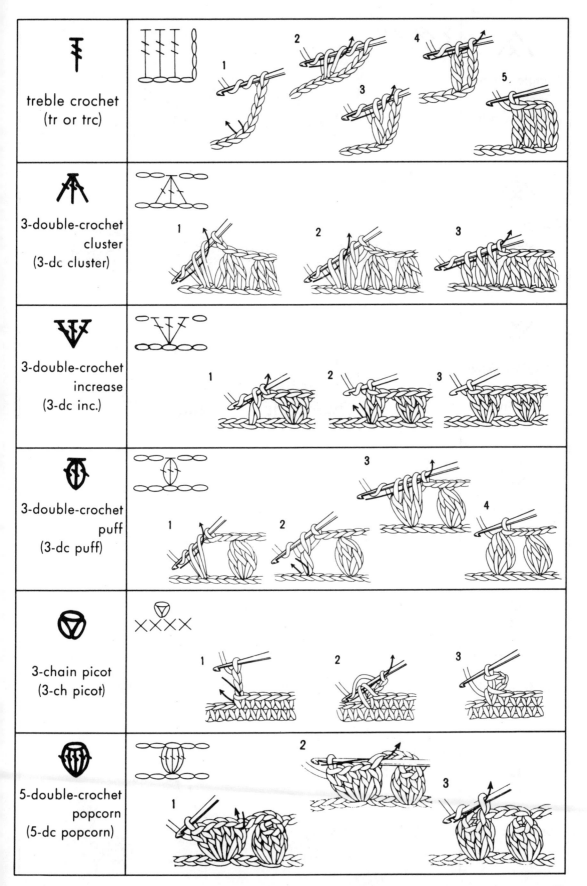

treble crochet (tr or trc)	
3-double-crochet cluster (3-dc cluster)	
3-double-crochet increase (3-dc inc.)	
3-double-crochet puff (3-dc puff)	
3-chain picot (3-ch picot)	
5-double-crochet popcorn (5-dc popcorn)	

2-single-crochet cluster (2-sc cluster)	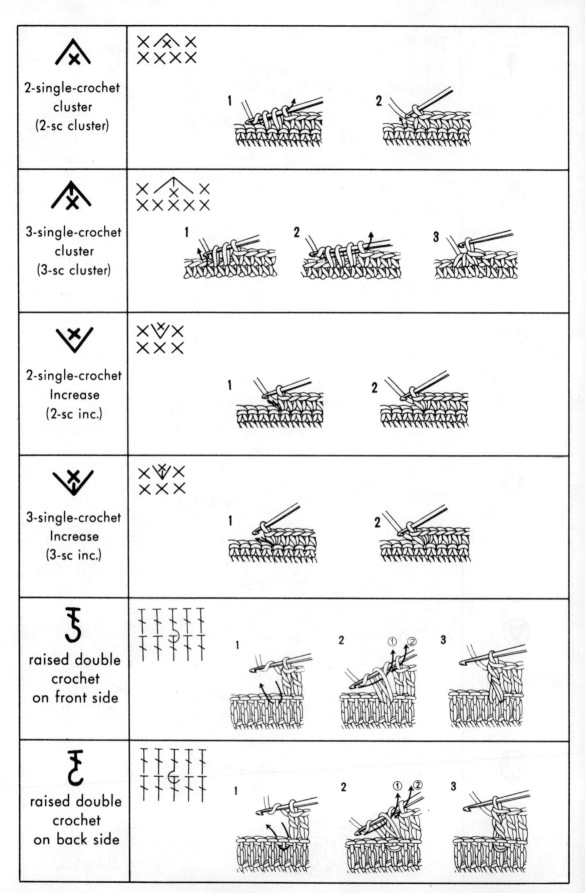
3-single-crochet cluster (3-sc cluster)	
2-single-crochet Increase (2-sc inc.)	
3-single-crochet Increase (3-sc inc.)	
raised double crochet on front side	
raised double crochet on back side	

HOW TO CROCHET MESH PATTERN

INCREASING:

*Increase at the beginning of row:

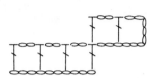 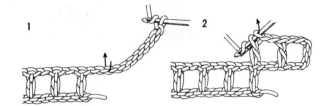

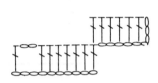 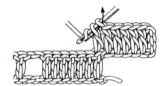

*Increase at the end of row:

(a) Inc 1 sp with dtr

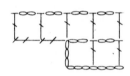 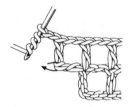

(b) Inc with ch sts added. Make a loop with new thread, insert hook in following to arrow, work foundation-ch (multiple of sps to inc).

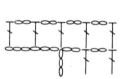 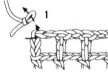 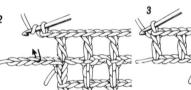 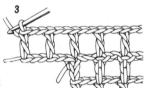

(c) Inc 1 st each with tr

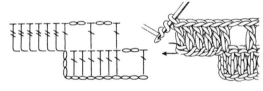

(d) Inc 1 st each with dc

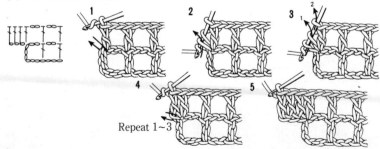

Repeat 1~3

BEGINNING

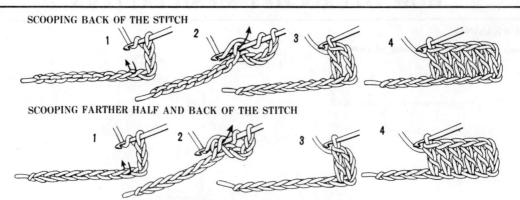

SCOOPING BACK OF THE STITCH

SCOOPING FARTHER HALF AND BACK OF THE STITCH

JOINING MOTIFS

JOINING WITH DRAW OUT STITCH (A)

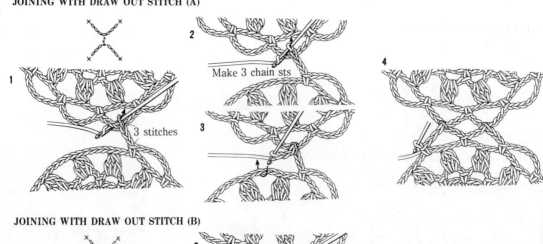

Make 3 chain sts

3 stitches

JOINING WITH DRAW OUT STITCH (B)

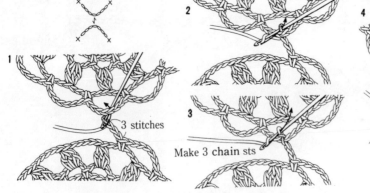

3 stitches

Make 3 chain sts

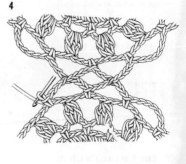

FINISHED IN OVERCAST

Join with half of stitch

Join with 1 stitch

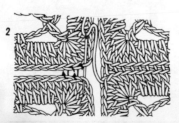